Quilting

Janet Wickell

TEACH YOURSELF BOOKS

Acknowledgements

I would like to thank Anne Knudsen at the Quilt Digest Press for recommending me to write this book, and the staff at Hodder & Stoughton for actually giving me the opportunity to do so. Everyone at the Publisher has been patient and helpful during the completion of this long distance project. As always, thanks to my family for their support whilst I worked on the manuscript and illustrations.

Dedication

To Carly Rebecca

For UK orders: please contact Bookpoint Ltd, 78 Milton Park, Abingdon, Oxon OX14 4TD. Telephone: (44) 01235 400414, Fax: (44) 01235 400454. Lines are open from 9.00 - 6.00, Monday to Saturday, with a 24 hour message answering service. Email address: orders@bookpoint.co.uk

For U.S.A. & Canada orders: please contact NTC/Contemporary Publishing, 4255 West Touhy Avenue, Lincolnwood, Illinois 60646-1975, USA. Telephone: (847) 679 5500, Fax: (847) 679 2494.

Long renowned as the authoritative source for self-guided learning – with more than 40 million copies sold worldwide – the Teach Yourself series includes over 200 titles in the fields of languages, crafts, hobbies, business and education.

British Library Cataloguing in Publication Data
A catalogue record for this title is available from The British Library.

Library of Congress Catalog Card Number: On file

First published in UK 2000 by Hodder Headline Plc, 338 Euston Road, London, NW1 3BH.

First published in US 2000 by NTC/Contemporary Publishing, 4255 West Touhy Avenue, Lincolnwood (Chicago), Illinois 60646 – 1975 USA.

The 'Teach Yourself' name and logo are registered trade marks of Hodder & Stoughton Ltd.

Copyright © 2000 Janet Wickell

Cover photo: Steve Tanner
Typeset by Wearset, Boldon, Tyne and Wear
Printed in Dubai, U.A.E. for Hodder & Stoughton Educational, a division of Hodder Headline Plc, 338 Euston Road, London NW1 3BH by Oriental Press.

Impression number   10 9 8 7 6 5 4 3 2 1
Year   2005 2004 2003 2002 2001 2000

Contents

Introduction

What is a quilt?

A quilt is an object made by placing a filling between two layers of fabric. The top and back layers of fabric can be made from one piece of cloth or many, and the filling is usually made from either cotton, wool, or synthetic fibres. The components are held in place with a running stitch sewn through the layers, or with ties made at intervals across the quilt. Although quilts can be utilitarian, hastily constructed to provide warmth, most quilts made today are an expression of the creativity of their makers.

Quilting has been traced back to ancient times, but became more common after the eleventh century. In addition to its importance for bedding, quilting was used to make warm garments, especially in areas with cold winters. Europeans brought their quilting skills to the New World but, although written references can be found for those early quilts, no examples have survived.

As fabrics became more readily available quilting continued to grow in popularity, due in part to the need for warm bed coverings but also because it was a way for quilters to create something beautiful for their surroundings. That desire continues today, with quiltmakers everywhere contributing their own styles to make this such a diverse craft. New techniques and methods are developed every day, and are passed on to quiltmakers around the world via the Internet. There's never been a time when members of the quilting community have been able to share their skills so quickly, and with such ease. This is a wonderful time to join the ranks of quilters, one of the friendliest and most supporting groups on Earth.

Types of quilts

Although there is an endless number of variations of each type, most quilts fall into three basic categories:

- patchwork
- appliqué
- whole cloth.

Patchwork quilts

These are the most popular type of quilt. Patchwork variations are made by sewing individual pieces of fabric together to create a design. They can be assembled by working in smaller sections, called **blocks**, or by sewing patches of fabric into a large quilt with an all-over design.

Appliqué quilts

To make an appliqué quilt, smaller pieces of fabric are sewn or fused to a larger background fabric. The background can be one large piece of cloth, or smaller blocks sewn together in rows.

Whole-cloth quilts

These quilts are made from one large piece of fabric. No patchwork or appliqué is included. Whole-cloth quilts rely solely on quilting motifs for embellishment.

Finished size and unfinished size

Patterns often use the terms **finished size** and **unfinished size**. Finished size refers to the dimensions of a patch or block after it is sewn to all its neighbours. Unfinished dimensions include seam allowances on each side of the unit – its size before any sewing takes place.

Seam allowances

If you use Imperial measurements, the standard seam allowance used in quiltmaking is $\frac{1}{4}$". Except for some appliqué techniques, all patch dimensions stated in this book assume you will use $\frac{1}{4}$" seams, and that allowance has been added to cutting instructions. Imperial measurements are given in parentheses after the metric units.

If you use the metric system, the patch sizes given in this book include an allowance for 7.5 mm seams. A 7.5 mm seam allowance is not a straight conversion from inches: it is the starting point for an entirely separate set of dimensions that allows you to make accurate cuts with metric rotary rulers. Refer to page 35 for instructions on how to set up your sewing machine to sew a 7.5 mm seam.

Quilters' tools and supplies

Each quiltmaker has favourite tools, many of which have been improvised from household objects such as freezer paper, which is used for many quilting tasks. That's why so many special tools are available – innovative quilters saw a need for something, and developed ways to fill that need. Over time you will accumulate a set of favourite tools, based on the way you make your own quilts. Start out with the basics, and grow from there.

Cutting tasks

- Rotary cutter, mat and rulers
- Sharp, all-purpose shears
- Appliqué scissors with pointed tips
- Paper scissors

Marking

- H or 2H (US #3 or #4) lead pencils
- White or yellow marking pencils
- Chalk or soapstone markers

Templates

- Freezer paper, gridded or plain
- Tracing paper or newsprint
- Carbon paper and tracing wheel

Piecing

- Sewing machine
- Machine needles
- Cotton fabrics and threads
- Fine seam ripper
- Long, fine, straight pins
- Iron and ironing board
- Hand-sewing needles

Finishing

- Batting
- Brass or stainless steel safety pins
- Darning needle for basting
- Thimble to fit middle finger of quilting hand
- Cotton quilting thread
- Nylon filament for machine quilting
- Walking and darning feet for machine quilting
- Betweens for hand quilting

Miscellaneous

- Value filter
- Hot iron transfer pen
- Graph paper
- Beeswax

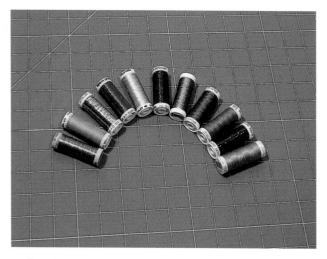

■ Spools of thread

■ Templates

Fabric basics

An understanding of the basic properties of fabric is an important tool, one you'll use every time you make a quilt. The knowledge will help you to understand why certain cuts of fabric work best in specific situations. And it puts you in control, giving you the confidence to design a quilt from scratch or to change any pattern to suit your needs.

Fabric grain

Patterns often mention the **straight-of-grain** – also called simply **straight grain** – which refers to the direction parallel to the threads in a piece of woven cloth. Fabric actually contains two straight grains, woven at right angles to each other.

- The **lengthwise grain** is made up of a series of side-by-side **warp** threads, which are secured to the loom during the weaving process.
- The **crosswise grain** is formed as **weft** threads are woven back and forth along the length of the warp.

The interlacing of threads in the straight grains holds the cloth together. Both grains add strength to fabric, but the lengthwise grain is sturdier.

Before weaving, the lengthwise threads are pulled tightly, then firmly attached to the ends of the loom, so very little stretch remains in them after the cloth is complete. The crosswise threads aren't pulled to their full capacity during weaving, which means they can stretch a little more after the cloth is woven.

There are usually more lengthwise threads than crosswise threads per square cm (inch) of fabric.

Two other fabric terms are important to quilters:

- **True bias** is defined as a 45° angle to the straight grain, but we refer to any angled cut as a **bias cut**. There are no stabilising threads running at an angle in cloth, so bias-cut edges are very stretchy.
- **Selvages** are the tightly bound edges along the fabric's outermost lengthwise grain. They are removed before patches are cut.

Selvage

Bias

Crosswise Grain

Lengthwise Grain

Selvage

Stretch test

This simple stretch test will help you to understand the differences in fabric grain.

1 Cut a 5 cm × 5 cm (2" × 2") square of fabric with edges parallel to the straight grains. If the thread direction is difficult to determine, turn the fabric over. It is sometimes easier to see threads on the reverse side.
2 Hold on to opposite sides of the square and tug. Pull again from the other opposite sides. Did you notice more stretch in one direction? That was the crosswise grain, and even though it stretched slightly, if you didn't pull too hard the square probably retained its shape.
3 Now pull on the square from corner to corner, along the bias. It probably stretched quite a bit, and may have become permanently distorted, this is because no stabilising threads run in that direction.

Understanding the differences in fabric grain will help you to assemble quilts with more ease and greater accuracy. You'll find that patches with edges cut along either straight grain are less likely to stretch out of shape, while bias edges must be handled with care to avoid distortion. There are references to fabric grain throughout this book, but a few basic guidelines for its placement are given on the following page.

- Properties of fabric

■ To minimise stretch, patch edges that lie on the outer perimeter of a block should be cut on the straight grain. Squares and rectangles are easy to cut, because their sides are at 90° to each other, matching the arrangement of straight-grain threads. However, triangles have at least one angled edge, which means at least one stretchy bias cut. Before cutting triangles or other angled-edge patches, analyse their position in the block to see which edges should lie on the straight grain.

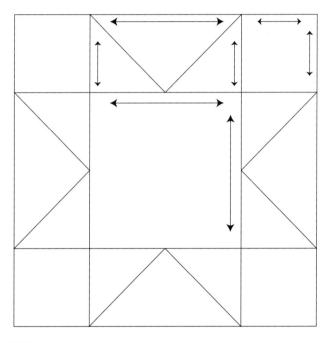

■ The arrows show the placement of the straight grain

■ Strips with sturdy, lengthwise grain edges make excellent borders and sashing. They help to anchor the outer pieced edges of blocks, which sometimes become distorted from handling by the time the quilt is assembled.
■ Bias cuts can be helpful too. A bias binding stretches to curve gracefully around a quilt with scalloped edges. Bias strips are the best choice for thin vines that wind around floral motifs on an appliqué quilt, or to mimic leading in a stained glass quilt.

Understanding the basic properties of fabric will give you the confidence to make layout decisions when you design a quilt or when you change a pattern to suit your needs. At times you might need to make an off-grain cut to take advantage of a design in the fabric. When that happens, you'll know to handle the piece with care. Knowing which types of cuts work best in different situations puts you in control of any cutting task.

Did you know?

You can stabilise an off-grain cut by backing the patch with sheer, fusible interfacing.

Cotton fabric

100% cotton fabrics are the preferred choice of quilters. Some fabrics may appear to be all-cotton, but actually contain synthetic fibres such as polyester. Check the label on the bolt, or ask a salesperson if you aren't sure. Although occasionally you may wish to use other types of fabric, there are many reasons why 100% cotton is the quilter's all-time favourite.

■ Cottons fray less than synthetic blends.
■ Cotton fabrics can be pressed flat, and they hold a crease. Synthetics don't press crisply, and sometimes tend to puff out or hold wrinkles where you don't want them.
■ Cottons are usually less transparent than synthetics, so underlying seam allowances are not as visible from the front side of the quilt.
■ Cotton fabrics tend to adhere to each other, while synthetic blends are often slippery, making it more difficult to match and sew patches accurately.
■ Cotton is soft, drapes nicely, and is easier to hand quilt than most synthetic fabrics. Cotton softens even more with age.
■ Cotton is the perfect choice for bed quilts, because its natural fibres breathe, wicking moisture away from the body. Synthetic fabrics block moisture, and hold in more warmth than is comfortable for a good night's sleep.

fabric basics

Choose tightly woven fabrics, with no large gaps between threads. Limp, loose weaves are more difficult to cut accurately, and produce patches with easily frayed edges. Making a quilt involves a lot of time and effort, so use the best fabrics you can afford. You won't be disappointed with the final product when you sew with good quality fabrics.

Is your fabric 100% cotton?

You may find a box of old fabric, or a friend may give you fabric as a gift. This simple burn test (see page 5) will help you determine whether a fabric is 100% cotton. Be sure to test outside, or in a well ventilated area.

■ Fabrics for quilting can include cotton, wool and synthetic fibres. Many quilters prefer 100% cotton fabrics

1 Clip off a small patch of fabric, approximately 4 cm (1½"). Place it in a fireproof container (such as an ashtray). Ignite a corner of the fabric with a match and pay attention to the odour of the smoke.

2 If the smoke smells like burning paper, the fabric is probably cotton. If it smells like chemicals, or burning plastic, synthetic fibres are present. An odour similar to burned hair indicates silk or wool content.

3 Examine the cooled ashes. Cotton ashes are fine and turn to soft dust when touched. Small, hard, irregular lumps are the remains of melted synthetic threads. Black, brittle beads indicate wool fibres.

4 If you still aren't sure, unravel a clump of threads from another small swatch of the fabric. Hold the clump with tweezers and slowly move a lit match towards it. Cotton fibres ignite as the match nears: synthetic fibres curl away from the heat.

If you love a fabric, but discover it isn't all cotton, do go ahead and use it. There's no rule that you *must* sew with one type of fabric or another. Recognising fabric content is just another aid to assembling the quilt, and to caring for it properly when it is complete.

Choosing needles and threads

Thread strength should be less than the strength of the fabric it is sewn to. When thread is stronger than fabric, it will eventually cut through the cloth along seam lines. This is especially true of polyester and cotton-wrapped polyester threads, which are not only strong, but also contain abrasive fibres. A compatible choice for sewing quilting cottons is 50/3 cotton thread. The 50 designates thickness, and the 3 indicates how many plies, or strands, of thread are twisted together. A 60/3 thread is another good choice, but more difficult to find in some areas. When you shop for thread remember two things: (1) the higher the first number, the finer the thread; (2) strength increases as the number of plies increases.

An 80/12 universal machine needle is compatible with both the 50/3 and 60/3 thread. Using the correct needle and thread is one way to make sure your quilts will be as beautiful in 50 years as they are the day you finish them.

Caring for cotton fabrics

Prewashing

Quilters have different opinions about whether or not to prewash their fabrics. There's no right or wrong decision – it's just a matter of personal choice. Use a gentle, non-phosphate soap, such as Orvus paste, to wash your fabrics. Many textile manufacturers currently recommend using water no hotter than room temperature.

Washing removes sizing and other chemicals

Manufacturers add coatings that stiffen fabric. The extra firmness makes rotary cutting easier because limp fabric tends to move around more under the cutter. Stiffer fabric is also easier to mark with pens or pencils when you need to trace around templates. The coatings usually include a chemical that helps prevent fading, so if your fabric is stored in a brightly lit room, leaving it unwashed helps the colours stay true.

If you are sensitive to chemicals, it might be better to prewash. Stiffness can be reintroduced by spraying on starch or sizing when it's time to use the fabric. That does add a chemical to the fabric again, but at least you can read the label to know exactly what's in it.

Washing shrinks cotton fabric

Natural fibres, including cotton, all have a tendency to relax, as they try to return to a position similar to the one in which they grew. During the weaving process threads are stretched, and protective coatings added to the finished cloth help keep threads from shifting. Washing removes some of the coatings, allowing the fibres to relax – which is what we see as shrinkage. Most shrinkage occurs during the first wash, but it can continue in future washings as more coatings are removed from the cloth.

Did you know?

A method used by quilters to make a new quilt resemble an antique is to assemble it with unwashed fabrics. When the quilt is complete (including batting, quilting, and binding), it is washed. Puckers form where fabric shrinks, which gives the impression of a vintage quilt. If you sew with unwashed cottons, keep in mind that the fabrics may shrink at different rates, and cause uneven puckering. Combining unwashed cottons with prewashed cottons isn't recommended, because it nearly always results in unbalanced puckering.

Washing alerts you to fabrics that bleed

Some fabrics **bleed** (lose their dyes). Bleeding isn't too much of a problem with modern quilting cottons, but does occur occasionally, particularly in dark-coloured fabrics. Colours can transfer from one fabric to another in the wash, or along seam lines where fabrics are sewn snugly to each other.

Test for bleeding

Submerge small squares of fabric in soapy water. Rinse, then dry the squares on light-coloured fabric or paper towelling. Did the dyes transfer onto the light fabric? If they did, try setting the dyes with a product such as *Retayne*, used by home dyers. Test again before using the fabric in the quilt.

Preventing colour transfer

Use *Synthrapol* when you wash fabrics or quilts. Adding a small amount of this liquid to the regular wash will help keep dyes suspended in water, rather than allowing them to deposit on other fabrics. Remove fabrics or quilts from the washer as soon as the cycle ends. Dry immediately.

Crocking

Crocking occurs when unset dyes on the surface of fabric flake off and transfer to other fabrics. It is common but sometimes not permanent. Test for crocking by wrapping a small piece of white fabric around your finger and rubbing it against the fabric you wish to check. This dry test can be done in the shop, before you purchase the fabric. If the amount of colour rubbed off is excessive, you might want to avoid that fabric. Crocking is usually reduced by prewashing the fabric.

Did you know?

Chlorinated water can cause otherwise stable fabrics to fade. If you notice that clothing seems to fade easily after a few washes, chlorine may be the culprit. To correct the problem add a product to the wash, used to neutralise chlorine in fish tanks, available in pet shops.

Storing fabrics

Shelving units make good storage bins for full-time sewing rooms. Seal wood shelves to keep acidic oils from contacting the fabric, or line shelves with a layer of aluminium foil. Fold fabrics or wrap into rolls, then stack on top of each other. Protect your fabrics from light by draping sheets over the shelving units when you're not sewing. You can make a more attractive light shield by rigging window shades or blinds to the top of the shelves, and pulling them down when not in use.

Some quilters like to store fabrics in see-through plastic boxes, which are easy to tuck under a bed or in a cupboard if you have to pack fabrics away between sewing sessions. To avoid mildew, make sure the fabrics are completely dry before sealing boxes with a lid.

2

Selecting colours and fabrics

Give the same quilt pattern to three different quilters – and the end result will be three entirely different quilts! Your choice of fabrics and colours puts your own special signature on everything you make. Quilting cottons are available for any type of project you desire, from reproductions of vintage fabrics to bold, colour splashed contemporary prints. There's never been a better time to express yourself with cloth!

The colour guidelines you'll see here are just that, guidelines – not rules – for colour selection. There *are* no rules, but there are a few simple things you can do to help make choosing colours a bit less confusing. Remember that the most important things about colour and fabric choice are *your* tastes and the end result *you* want to achieve.

Using a colour wheel

A colour wheel is a tool for understanding the relationships between colours. The most commonly used wheel contains twelve colours, including the three **primary colours** of blue, yellow, and red, colours that cannot be created by mixing other colours. All colours on the wheel are referred to as **pure** colours, the most intense version of the colour.

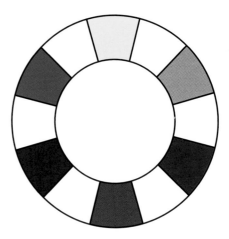

■ Adding Secondary Colours

Mixing a primary and secondary colour goes a step further, creating the colour between them on the wheel, called a **tertiary** colour.

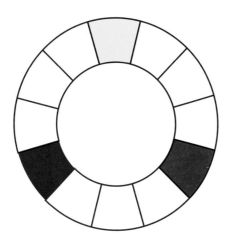

■ Primary Colours

Primary colours are spaced at equal distances around the wheel. When two primary colours are mixed in equal amounts, the result is the colour midway between them, called a **secondary** colour. Blue and red mixed equally makes violet; yellow and blue make green; yellow and red make orange.

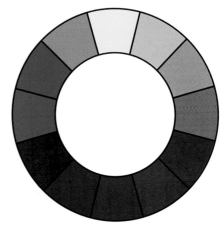

■ Adding Tertiary Colours

Neutral colours

Black, white and grey are all **neutral** colours, because they contain no colour. Light beige is considered a neutral, even though it contains colour. Neutrals make good backgrounds, and tend to soften colours placed next to them.

Colour value

Value refers to how dark or light a colour is. Any colour can be made darker by adding black, which produces a **shade** of the pure colour. If white is added, the colour becomes a lighter **tint** of the original. Another term you might see is **tone**, which is what colours are called when grey is added to them.

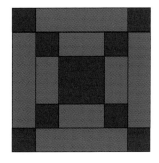

■ Warm colours advance forward

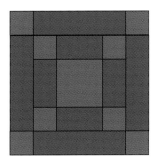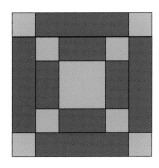

■ Similar versus contrasting values

Value is important to quiltmakers because the contrast between fabrics of different values is what defines our patterns. When same-value fabrics are placed side-by-side, they blend into each other. There will be times when a blended look is what you are trying to achieve, but perhaps more times when you want a clearly defined pattern to emerge.

It's fairly easy to sort same-colour fabrics from light to dark, but sorting becomes a little trickier when additional colours are added to the mix. In part this is usually because you've added **colour warmth** to the mixture. The colour wheel can be split in half, with blues and greens on one side (considered **cool**), and oranges and reds on the opposite side (considered **warm**). Warm colours come forward in the quilt design, popping out in such a way that we often notice them first.

The relative colour warmth of a fabric varies depending on the fabric it is placed next to. For instance, a violet print appears warm when placed next to green, but the same fabric appears cool when placed next to bright red.

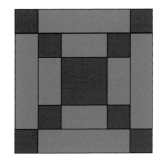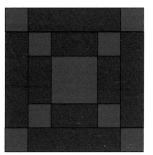

■ Relative colour warmth

There are several ways of sorting fabrics by value:

■ Sort fabrics close-up, moving from light to dark. Tack them to a neutral wall in the same order. Step back to view the assortment from a distance. Do fabrics still appear to blend from light to dark, or do some pop out at you?
■ Look at fabrics through a peephole, the kind of magnifier used to see who is knocking on your door before you open it. For a better image, turn the viewer around to make the fabrics appear further away.

- Make black and white photocopies of fabric swatches, then sort the paper copies. It is usually easier to determine value when colour is eliminated (but you'll still need to consider warmth).
- Look at fabrics through a value filter, which also masks colour.

Remember that the terms 'light', 'medium', and 'dark' depend on the starting point for your quilt. A dark-blue fabric appears quite dark when sewn next to a light blue, but may appear to be medium in value when sewn next to a black fabric.

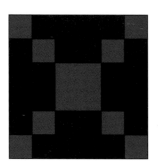

■ Value is determined by neighbouring fabrics

Did you know?

Adding small amounts of a very dark shade, and a very light tint, is sometimes all it takes to turn a 'ho-hum' quilt into a fantastic design.

Colour harmonies

The colour wheel can help you to devise colour plans based on the relationships between colours, called **colour harmonies**.

One-colour harmony, or monochromatic

This colour scheme uses just one colour. Neutral fabrics such as white, off-white, grey and black can be included too, because they do not add colour.

For one-colour quilts, it's important to include a variety of contrast and scale among fabrics.

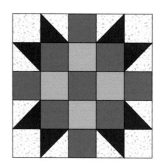

■ One-colour layout

Analogous colour harmonies

An analogous colour scheme combines colours that lie side-by-side on the colour wheel. This type of arrangement produces colours with a natural harmony, because they have a colour in common with their neighbours. Select three or five adjacent colours.

To provide an accent to this type of an arrangement, add small amounts of a colour that lies opposite the group on the colour wheel.

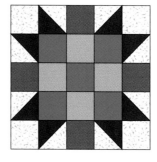

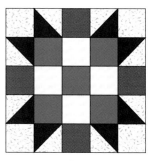

■ Add 'pizzazz' to side-by-side layouts with small amounts of an opposite colour

Opposite colour harmonies

Colours directly across from each other on the colour wheel are called opposite colours. Colours such as these are also called **complementary colours**. One often completes the other, because it is mixed from a primary colour different from the first, and brings into the mix what the other lacks. It is often best to use unequal amounts of complementary colours.

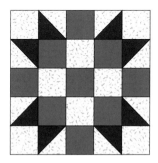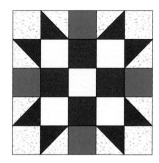

■ Opposite colour schemes

For more variety, use two colours and their opposites.

To accent this type of arrangement, add small amounts of a colour two steps away from one of the complementary colours. Accents can be used with any colour arrangement, and are usually best in small amounts, giving the quilt a little 'pizzazz' without overpowering the other colours.

These harmonies are just a small sampling of the ways you can mix colours successfully. Experimentation is the best way to become more comfortable using a variety of colours in your quilts, and will give you the confidence to follow your instincts.

Scrap quilts

Making a scrappy quilt is a great way to play with colours. They can be made with just a few colours, or can contain colours from around the wheel.

1   Sort fabrics by colour, rather than from light to dark. Add and subtract fabrics to make side-by-side colours blend. Choose pure colours, shades, tints and tones. Sort and re-sort until the fabrics seem to melt into each other. If there are gaps where colours just won't blend, try adding neutrals to form a bridge from one fabric to another.

2   Once you've completed step 1 sort the fabrics by value, from light to dark. Determine which design elements in the quilt should be sewn from light fabrics, and which need darks and mediums. Cut patches for the quilt based on those needs, ignoring colour completely.

3   Assemble the quilt without regard to colour placement, choosing fabrics in a random manner, depending on the value you need for a patch. As the fabrics blended together in step 1, they will blend together when the quilt is complete.

Did you know?

A Charm Quilt is the ultimate scrap quilt. No fabric is used for more than one piece.

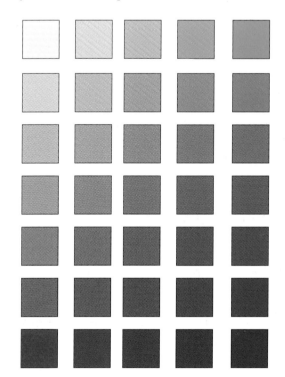

■ Sorting fabrics

Design walls

During the design phase, it's helpful to place quilt components on a wall, so that you can step back to see an overall view of the layout. Tack a large piece of flannel to any wall to make a quick design wall. Unless they are very heavy, components stick to the flannel without having to be pinned, which helps you to make changes quickly and easily.

Before you sew the quilt together, leave the room for a while. When you come back, you'll see the quilt with a fresh outlook, which is often just what's needed for a few last minute improvements.

Using printed fabrics

Most quilters use 100% cotton fabrics, so the actual woven textures of the fabrics in a quilt are identical. Imagine how a quilt would look if plain muslin were cut apart and re-sewn into a patchwork design – probably not too interesting. Varying colour is one way to add interest, but to keep quilts from looking 'flat' you must introduce visual texture by including a wide variety of fabrics printed in a variety of scales or print sizes.

■ Florals can soften a layout

Floral prints

Visit any quilt shop and the first thing you'll notice is that most of the prints are florals. Florals are probably the most popular type of fabric. You'll find examples ranging from small calico designs to large, boldly coloured prints.

Stripes and plaids

You'll find stripes of all widths; some straight, some wavy. Stripes might flow in the direction of the fabric's straight grain, or they might move in line with the bias. Plaids can be found in the same variety too. Their crossed lines may be woven into the fabric, rather than printed on top of it. Stripes and plaids add movement to the quilt, especially if cut slightly off grain for a 'tilted' appearance.

■ Geometric prints add visual interest

Geometric prints

These fabrics are based on geometric designs such as dots, circles, squares, and triangles. Printed motifs can be random, or flow together in a structured arrangement.

■ Stripes and plaids add movement

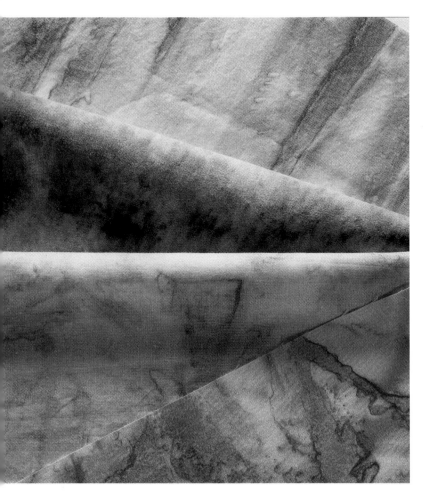

■ Use hand-dyed fabrics to add colour and random texture

Hand-dyed fabrics

The variations in hand-dyed fabrics are another good way to add texture. As with tone-on-tone prints, they provide the look of solids but have a little more visual interest.

Tone-on-tone prints

From a distance, tone-on-tone prints may appear solid. When you move closer, you'll find that they actually have a printed motif using variations of the same colour. These fabrics add a subtle visual texture that is lacking in solid-coloured fabrics.

■ Tone-on-tone prints add subtle texture

Conversational prints

A conversational print depicts a real thing. You've probably seen prints that depict scissors, little sewing machines, dogs and cats, horses, and birds. All of these are examples of conversational prints, which have always been popular with quilters.

When most of us shop for fabrics, we tend to buy things we like – but sometimes it's best to shop for things we *need*! Look at fabrics from a new perspective, and build your collection to include things you don't particularly like. You never know when a chartreuse green geometric print will add just the right bit of flash to a special quilt!

■ Conversational prints depicting 'real' objects

3

Drafting patchwork blocks

Ideas for quilts are everywhere – a gorgeous set of ceramic tiles might inspire you to mimic their layout in cloth; a motif on a building might be the perfect design for your next quilt. Learning a few basic drafting skills helps take the mystery out of block construction, whether you want to create an original design or make changes to an existing one.

Patchwork block layouts

Most patchwork quilt blocks are categorised by the number of equal squares – or **units** – they contain. All or part of each grid of squares can be subdivided into more squares, but the beginning framework for each type of block remains the same. With a little practice, you'll be able to analyse and draft any patchwork design.

Four-patch blocks initially contain four equal squares, two across and two down, but you will see many four-patch blocks with subdivided units.

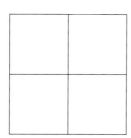  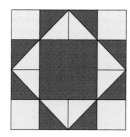

■ Four-patch blocks

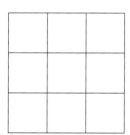 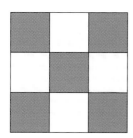 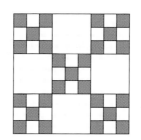

Nine-patch blocks initially contain nine equal squares, three across and three down. There are many nine-patch blocks with further divisions.

■ Nine-patch blocks

Two other patch types are named by how many grids are in their horizontal and vertical rows rather than by how many total grids they contain.

Five-patch blocks have a grid of five squares across and five down, or 25 squares.

Seven-patch blocks have a grid of seven squares across and seven down, or 49 squares. These blocks aren't usually divided into more units.

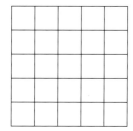 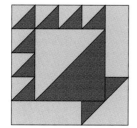

■ Five-patch blocks

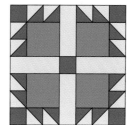

■ Seven-patch blocks

One-patch blocks contain a single, repeating shape. Two examples are the traditional Grandmother's Flower Garden and the Thousand Pyramids patterns. The components of these quilts, and a few other designs such as the eight-pointed star, do not fit into a gridded framework.

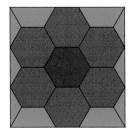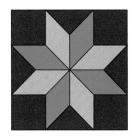

■ One-patch layouts

■ 'Zigzaggy' floral quilt

Selecting a block size

When you use templates to make a quilt, the individual units within blocks can be any size, because templates provide you with exact marking and cutting guides. When rotary-cutting methods are used (see Chapter 4), the smallest units in blocks should be in increments no less than the smallest divisions on your rotary ruler. For rulers marked in inches, this is usually $\frac{1}{8}$". Metric rulers are usually marked at 2.5 mm intervals.

An easy way to select a block size is to use a dimension that can be evenly divided by the number of grids within the block. For a five-patch block to finish at 25 cm (10") square, divide that measurement by the number of units per row: 5. The answer, 5 cm (2") per unit, is easy to rotary cut or draw as templates. Dimensions needn't be whole numbers. Fractions are fine, as long as those fractions are the intervals marked on your ruler.

The finished block size also depends on which measuring system you use. A 12" five-patch block isn't suitable for rotary cutting with imperial rulers, because the finished size of each of its units is 2.4", not a marked interval. But a five-patch block of 30 cm, approximately the same size, *would* work with metric rulers, because its units are each 6 cm, an easy-to-cut dimension.

Combining different blocks

To combine two or more different block types in a rotary-cut quilt, find a size that works for all. Four-patch and nine-patch blocks can be rotary cut to finish at 30 cm (12") square because units required for both are easy to cut when divided into that number. To add the same-size seven-patch block would be difficult, because the seven-patch units finish at a size we can't cut with rotary rulers: 4.3 cm (1.7"). If you can't find a common size to allow rotary cutting for all blocks, determine a size that works for most, and use templates to assemble the rest.

Did you know?

If the quilt must finish at a specific size, you can adjust its overall dimensions by altering the width of sashing or borders.

Drafting blocks

Choose a graph paper that works with the finished size of the units in the block. For instance, use four-grid per inch graph paper to draw units with $\frac{1}{4}$" or $\frac{1}{2}$" dimensions (use metric graph paper if you are cutting shapes in centimetres). Large sheets of graph paper can be purchased at office or art supply shops.

To draft a five-patch basket block of any size

■ A five-patch basket block

1   Draw a square equal to the finished size of the block (no seam allowances). Draw a grid within the square, five equal squares across and five down.

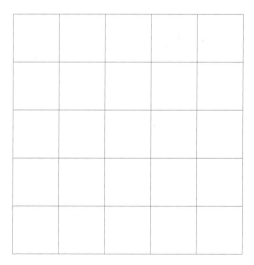

■ Draw the grid

2 Divide each square in the grid to match the units in the original pattern. Some of the patches in this block occupy more than one grid. Mark grain lines on each piece, placing the straight-of-grain on the outer perimeter of the block.

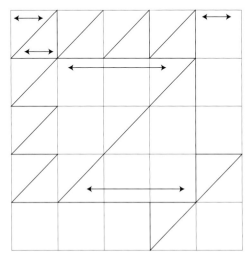

■ Mark grain placement

Drafting an eight-pointed star

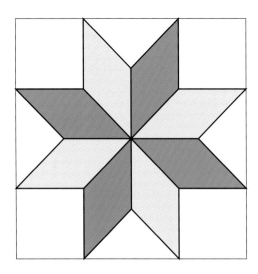

■ An eight-pointed star

Eight-pointed stars contain 45° diamonds in a grid of unequal divisions. You can use graph paper to help with outside lines, but divisions within the block will not usually fall on a grid. This method requires a sharp marker, paper, a straight edge, and a compass.

1 Draw a square the size of your finished star block. Mark diagonal lines from corner to corner. Draw straight lines to divide the square in half vertically and horizontally.

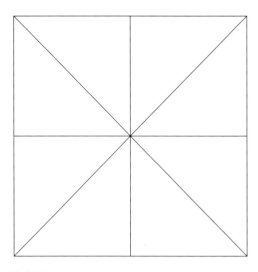

■ Mark segments

2 Place the point of the compass at the corner of the block. Open the compass until its pencil matches the centre of the square. Move in an arc, marking the two points where the arc intersects the outer edges of the square.

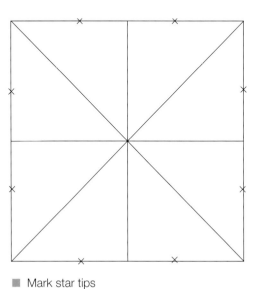

■ Mark star tips

Repeat marking points from each remaining corner. You will have eight marks along the outer edges of the square.

3 Draw straight lines to connect marks on opposite sides of the square.

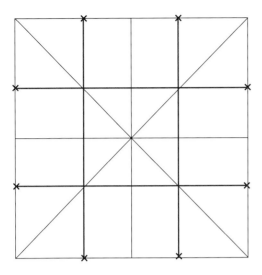

■ Connect marks

4 Draw diagonal lines to connect marks at a 45° angle to each other. Use the edge of a pencil to colour-in diamonds if it helps you to see their shape. Mark grain placement on patches, placing the straight grain parallel to the outer edges of the block.

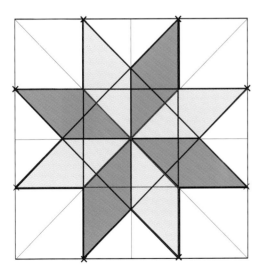

■ Connect marks diagonally

Drafting tips

- Use the finished size drawing to construct templates, adding a 7.5 mm ($\frac{1}{4}$") seam allowance around each shape to calculate the cut size.
- Analyse patches for rotary cutting. Chapter 5 shows you how to determine seam allowances and strip widths for specific shapes.
- Are there methods that will speed up assembly? Triangle squares (see page 51) in the basket block can be pieced quickly and accurately using quick-piecing methods.

4

Cutting patchwork shapes

R otary cutting may be
one of the most
important additions to the
quilting world, because it
allows us to cut very accurate
pieces for our quilts in record
time. However, there will be
times when a traditional
scissors cut is the best way
to accomplish a task.
Become familiar with all of the
marking and cutting options
so that you can choose the
one that's best for you.

Rotary-cutting basics

Rotary cutting allows you to cut patches without premarking their shapes on fabric. This technique is one of the most versatile and time-saving skills a quilter can master. Rotary skills will also improve your cutting accuracy, since sides of shapes are sliced in one continuous motion rather than in shorter, choppy scissors cuts.

Rotary cutters

Rotary cutters resemble pizza cutters, with an important difference – their blades are razor sharp. Blades come in three diameters: 28, 45, and 60 mm. Small blades are good for cutting around curved shapes. Larger blades are the best choice for all-purpose use. Replace the blade when it no longer makes a clean cut through the cloth.

Find a cutter that feels comfortable in your hand. Some have blades that retract automatically, others are fitted with a button or lever to move the blade in and out from beneath its guard. Ensure cutters and blades are kept well out of the reach of children, and to enable the blade guard after each cut.

Rotary mats

Special cutting mats protect surfaces from the rotary blade and help the blade to stay sharper for longer. Many mats are self-healing, which means that any grooves the blade leaves in the mat are not permanent. Some mats are reversible, allowing you to flip from a dark side to a light side and use whichever contrasts best with the fabric being cut. Mats are usually marked with a grid, which is a good guide for fabric placement but not accurate enough to measure strips for cutting. Because they warp, mats should be kept out of direct sunlight and away from heat sources.

Rotary rulers

Thick, acrylic, see-through rulers should be used when rotary cutting. Start with the basic rulers and add to your collection as you discover what works best for you. For cutting consistency, build your collection with rulers from the same manufacturer. Metric rulers should be marked with dimensions in 2.5 mm increments. Imperial rulers are usually marked at $\frac{1}{8}$" intervals. Sizes and markings vary by brand.

■ Rotary equipment

- A 16 cm × 60 cm (6" × 24") ruler is indispensable and will enable you to make nearly any type of cut. It should be marked with 30°, 45°, and 60° lines.
- A 16 cm × 16 cm (6" × 6") square is helpful for aligning and cutting squares and triangle squares. Dimensions are marked along two adjoining sides, with a 45° diagonal rule running through them.
- A 32 cm × 32 cm (15" × 15") square is great for squaring up large blocks and quilt corners, and for cutting setting squares and triangles and large background blocks for appliqué.

Other helpful rulers

- Shorter rulers are nice for cutting segments from strips.
- Narrow rulers, such as 12 cm × 36 cm (3" × 24"), are less bulky for making narrow cuts.
- There are hundreds of special rulers available to help you cut curves and specific shapes, such as diamonds, hexagons, and triangles. After a little experience you'll know which ones are important for your own quilting needs.

Cutting strips

Individual shapes are cut from parent strips of fabric with long edges parallel to the lengthwise or crosswise grain. If you are left-handed, the cuts you make, and the angled lines you use, will be mirror images of the ones illustrated. If your long ruler does not have criss-crossed angle lines, you might need to alter ruler placement.

Before cutting the first strip, the leading edge of the fabric must be squared up so that it is at a 90° angle to its base.

1 To cut crosswise grain strips, fold the fabric along its length, just as it came off the bolt. Press the fold when you're sure it is straight and pucker-free. If you are working on a small mat, you may need to fold the fabric again, making it four layers thick. Fold carefully, because each fold creates an opportunity for inaccuracies.

Did you know?

Lengthwise grain strips are less stretchy than crosswise grain strips. To cut them, fold the fabric crosswise at the midpoint of its length (shorten longer lengths for better accuracy).

2 Place the fabric on your mat with the fold near the bottom edge and the side to be squared on the left. Position a rotary ruler near the left end, aligning one of its horizontal lines to the fold. Place a long rotary ruler to the left of the first, so that the edges fit snugly against each other. The lines of both rulers should be parallel to the folded edge, and the right edge of the outer ruler should extend onto the fabric far enough to cover all layers.

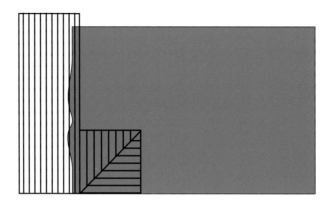

3 Carefully remove the right-side ruler, keeping your left hand on the long ruler to hold it in place. Roll the rotary cutter from bottom to top along the ruler's right edge. Spread your fingers out to hold the ruler securely, but take care to keep them out of the path of the cutter. You might need to move your fingers up the ruler as you cut. Discard the narrow strip of fabric you just cut away. The left edge of the material should now be at a 90° angle to the folded edge.

4 To cut strips from the squared-up edge, align the vertical line that matches your required strip width with the left edge of the fabric (make sure that the ruler is placed so that numbers increase from right to left). Match any horizontal line with the fold. Slide the cutter from bottom to top to separate the strip.

5 Open the strip to its full length and look at the area near the fold. If the strip has a bend in the middle, the fabric's leading edge was not at a 90° angle to the fold. Square up the end again before cutting more strips. It's common to have to re-square the end occasionally when you are cutting many strips, so don't think you are doing something wrong if the 'bend' pops up occasionally. It will happen less often if you are always careful to align a vertical rule with the edge of the fabric, and a horizontal rule with the fold.

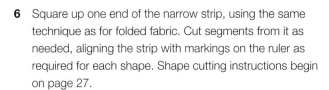

6 Square up one end of the narrow strip, using the same technique as for folded fabric. Cut segments from it as needed, aligning the strip with markings on the ruler as required for each shape. Shape cutting instructions begin on page 27.

Did you know?

Some people use only one ruler, and square up fabric from the right-hand side. Align a horizontal rule on your long ruler, with the fold near the right edge of fabric, then slice from bottom to top. Turn the fabric around carefully to keep the edges together, then cut strips from the left side as described. This right-side approach is a good way to square up the ends of individual strips. Try both methods to see which works best for you.

Rotary-cutting tips

- If you find it difficult to cut long strips accurately, work with smaller pieces of fabric until you are accustomed to the technique.
- Use spray starch or sizing to stiffen the fabric. This makes it easier to cut.
- Attach self-adhesive sandpaper or acrylic tabs to the bottom of your rulers to prevent them from slipping on the fabric.
- Always roll the rotary cutter away from your body.
- You can stack strips for cutting, but remember that the more strips you stack, the less accurate the resulting patches will be. Although it's more time consuming, I prefer to work with no more than two layers, especially for small pieces that have little room for error.
- Press layers together just before cutting. It helps them to stick to each other.

Cutting patchwork shapes

Nearly all patchwork shapes can be rotary cut from long parent strips of fabric. The dimensions in this book include a 7.5 mm seam allowance for quilters using metric dimensions and a $\frac{1}{4}$" seam allowance for those using the Imperial system.

Patchwork Shapes

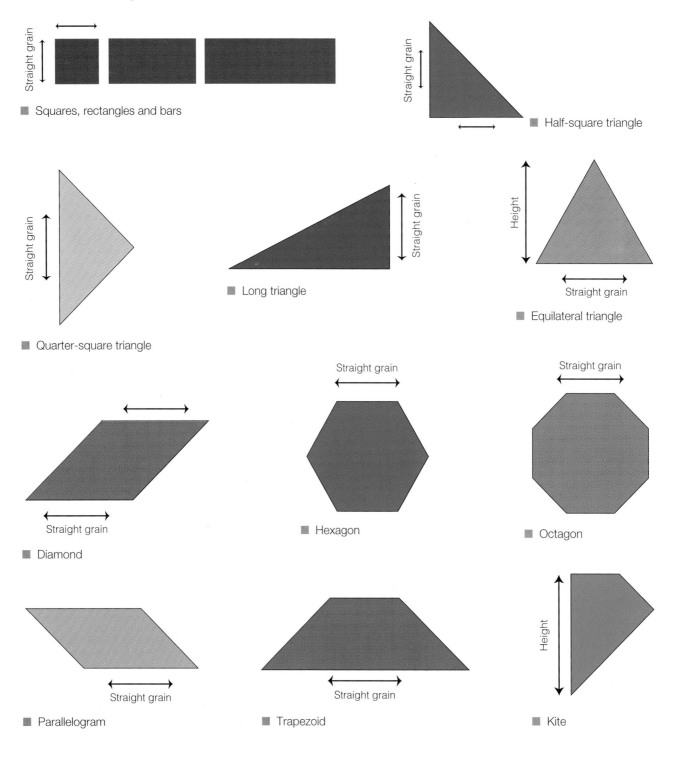

Straight grain

■ Squares, rectangles and bars

Straight grain

■ Half-square triangle

Straight grain

■ Quarter-square triangle

Straight grain

■ Long triangle

Height

Straight grain

■ Equilateral triangle

Straight grain

Straight grain

■ Diamond

Straight grain

■ Hexagon

Straight grain

■ Octagon

Straight grain

■ Parallelogram

Straight grain

■ Trapezoid

Height

■ Kite

Squares and rectangles

A **square** has four 90°, or right, angles and four equal sides. A true **rectangle** has four right angles and is twice as long as it is wide. Rectangles of different proportions are called **bars**. These shapes are used as starting points for other rotary-cut shapes.

To rotary cut squares and rectangles, cut straight-grain strips that are 1.5 cm ($\frac{1}{2}$") wider than the width of the finished patch, and then cut away segments that are 1.5 cm ($\frac{1}{2}$") longer than the finished length.

■ Rotary cutting squares, rectangles and bars

Triangles

A **triangle** has three angles and three sides. At least one edge is always cut on the fabric's stretchy bias, so handle triangles carefully to avoid stretch.

Half-square triangles

After squares, the **half-square triangle** is the most frequently used patchwork shape. It is cut by dividing a square in half once diagonally. The straight grain runs parallel to the triangle's short sides.

To rotary cut half-square triangles, cut a square with sides 2.5 cm ($\frac{7}{8}$") longer than the finished short sides of the triangle and then cut the square in half diagonally.

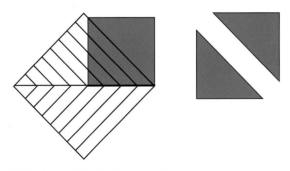

■ Rotary cutting half-square triangles

Quarter-square triangles

A **quarter-square triangle** looks exactly like a half-square triangle, but there's a big difference in its structure. This patch is cut by dividing a square twice diagonally to form four triangles with the straight grain along their longest edge. You will see them in many blocks, but their most common use is as setting triangles for on-point layouts, where they fill in the jagged outer edges of the quilt (see page 89).

To rotary cut four quarter-square triangles, cut a square with sides 3.5 cm ($1\frac{1}{4}$") longer than the finished length of the triangle's longest edge, and then cut the square in half twice diagonally.

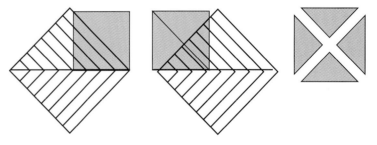

■ Rotary cutting quarter-square triangles

Did you know?

Beginning on page 51, you'll find quick-piecing instructions for half- and quarter-square triangle units. They show you how to assemble these popular units without cutting individual triangles.

Long triangles

A **scalene triangle** has three unequal sides. The variation used most often in quilting is the **right scalene triangle**, which quilters call the **long triangle**. Long triangles are cut by dividing a rectangle or bar diagonally from corner to corner. The straight grain runs parallel to the straight edges.

cutting patchwork shapes

Cutting long triangles from rectangles

1 Cut a strip of fabric 2 cm ($\frac{11}{16}$") wider than the finished length of the half rectangle's short side. Most rotary rulers aren't marked in increments that small, so estimate the distance as closely as possible.

2 Cut a rectangle from the strip that is 4 cm ($\frac{5}{16}$") longer than the finished length of the half rectangle. Align your rotary ruler to intersect opposite corners of the rectangle, then cut it in half diagonally to create two identical long triangles.

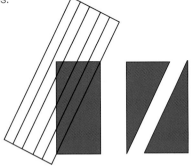

■ Rotary cutting long triangles from a rectangle

For long triangles that are a mirror image of this pair, slice a second rectangle along the opposite diagonal.

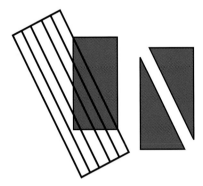

■ Cutting mirror images

Cutting long triangles from bars

To cut long triangles from bars, draw a finished-size triangle on graph paper. Add 7.5 mm ($\frac{1}{4}$") seam allowance to each side. Cut parent strips and bars to match the length and width of this triangle, then divide diagonally.

Equilateral triangles

An **equilateral triangle** has a 60° angle at each corner and measures the same length along each of its three sides. To rotary cut equilateral triangles follow the steps below.

1 To find the finished height of an equilateral triangle, measure the distance from the midpoint of one side to the tip of the angle above it. Add 2.25 cm ($\frac{3}{4}$") to the finished height to calculate the parent strip width.

2 Align the 60° line of a long rotary ruler with the bottom right edge of a parent strip. Cut along the right edge of the ruler to establish a 60° cut edge on the fabric. Discard the cut end.

■ Rotary cutting equilateral triangles – step 2

3 Rotate the ruler, aligning its other 60° line with the bottom edge of the strip. The top right edge of the ruler should intersect the top edge of the first cut. Cut along the right side of the ruler to separate the first triangle. To cut more, continue moving the ruler back and forth between the 60° lines. The leg length of cut triangles should measure 2.5 cm ($\frac{7}{8}$") longer than their finished size.

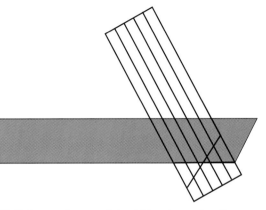

■ Rotary cutting equilateral triangles – step 3

Diamonds

A **diamond** is a flattened square. It has four sides of equal length, but the corner angles have changed. Quilt patterns contain 30°, 45°, and 60° diamonds, with the degree designation referring to the angles at their narrow points. All three diamond types are cut from parent strips that are 1.5 cm (½") wider than the finished height of the diamond.

1 Align the 30°, 45°, or 60° line on the ruler with the left lower edge of the fabric. Slide the ruler far enough onto the strip so that its upper edge extends slightly past the fabric's top corner. Cut along the right edge of the ruler to establish the angle.

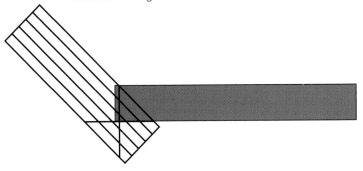

■ Rotary cutting diamonds – step 1

2 Locate the line on your rotary ruler that matches the cutting height of the diamond – the same line that is used to cut parent strips. Match the line to the angled left edge of the fabric, and align the degree line with the bottom edge of the strip. Roll the cutter along the right side of the ruler to cut a diamond.

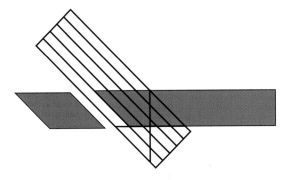

■ Rotary cutting diamonds – step 2

Hexagons

Hexagons are 60° diamonds that have ! narrow points.

1 Cut a parent strip 1.5 cm (½") wider than t! the hexagon. Cut a 60° diamond from the strip (see above).

2 Place the diamond on the mat with its long, narrow tips pointing to the sides. Find the ruler line that equals half of the diamond's cutting height, and align it vertically to pass through the top and bottom points of the diamond. Align the 60° line with the diamond's lower right edge. Trim away the point on the right side of the ruler. Rotate the shape 180° and trim the opposite point.

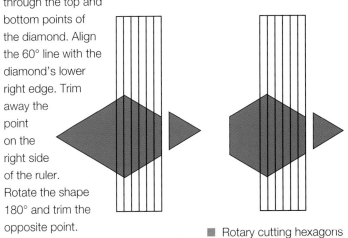

■ Rotary cutting hexagons

Octagons

Octagons have eight equal sides and 135° angles at their points. Cut this shape by trimming the four corners from a square.

1 Cut a parent strip 1.5 cm (½") wider than the finished height of the octagon. Cut a square from the parent strip.

2 Turn the square over and draw two diagonal lines to make an 'X' on the fabric. Place the square wrong-side up on the mat, with the corners pointing up and down. Locate the ruler line that equals half of the square's cutting height, and align it with the vertical line on the square. Align any horizontal rule with the horizontal line on the square. Trim the right point.

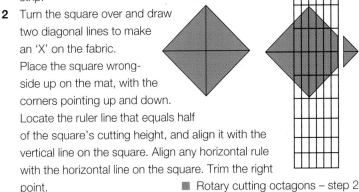

■ Rotary cutting octagons – step 2

3 Rotate the patch 180° and trim the opposite point. Trim the two remaining points in the same way. Measure the distance between opposite straight edges – all four dimensions should be the same.

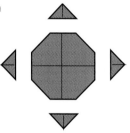

■ Rotary cutting octagons – step 3

45° Parallelograms

Parallelograms resemble stretched diamonds. The opposite legs are the same length, but one pair is shorter than the other.

1 Cut a parent strip 1.5 cm (½") wider than the parallelogram's finished height. Cut the left end of the strip at 45° as if you were preparing the strip to cut 45° diamonds.

2 Add 2.25 cm (¾") to the finished length of the parallelogram. Beginning at the narrow angle, measure and mark this distance on the top edge of the fabric. Align the 45° line with the bottom of the strip, and a long line on the ruler with the angled edge of the fabric. If the angled edge falls between ruler lines, keep the edge an equal distance between lines. Cut along the right side of the ruler.

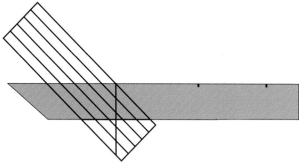

■ Rotary cutting a parallelogram

Trapezoids

Trapezoids are rectangles with two ends trimmed at an angle. The ends can be cut at any angle, but most trapezoids used in quilting have 45° ends.

1 Cut a parent strip that is 1.5 cm (½") wider than the finished height of the trapezoid.

2 Trim the strip's left edge at a 45° angle. Add 3.5 cm (1¼") to the finished length of the trapezoid's longest edge. Measure and mark this distance across the top of the strip, beginning at the piece's narrow tip.

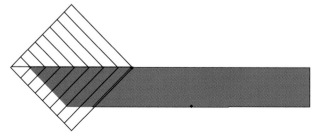

■ Rotary cutting trapezoids – step 2

3 Turn the ruler, and align the opposite 45° line with the bottom of the strip. Cut another 45° angle to intersect the pencil mark, making the angled edge a mirror image of the first.

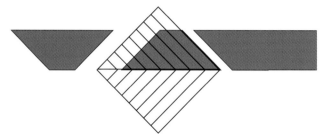

■ Rotary cutting trapezoids – step 3

Kites

Kites are half-square triangles with trimmed sides. Eight 135° kites form an octagon when sewn together along their long edges.

1 To calculate parent strip width, add 2.5 cm (⅞") to the finished height of the kite. Cut a square of that dimension from the parent strip, then cut the square in half diagonally.

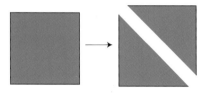

■ Rotary cutting kites – step 1

2 Place one of the triangles on the mat, its long, bias edge up. Place the line used to cut the parent strips directly on the left tip of the triangle. Align the top of the ruler with the triangle's long edge. Cut along the ruler's right edge. Repeat to trim the second triangle.

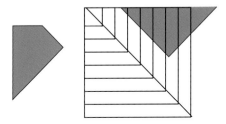

■ Rotary cutting kites – step 2

Cutting odd-sized pieces

Make paper guides for pieces that can't be accurately measured with rotary equipment. Draw the shape on paper and add 7.5 mm ($\frac{1}{4}$") seam allowance around all sides. Tape the shape to your rotary ruler with removable tape and use it as a guide when cutting strips and segments.

Cutting with templates

Templates are exact copies of pattern pieces. They are used to mark fabric for cutting. Even though rotary-cutting methods have diminished the need for templates, you will encounter patterns where they will help you to piece a block with more ease.

- Odd-sized blocks may contain patches with dimensions that cannot be accurately rotary cut.
- You might wish to target a specific area of a printed fabric.
- Templates allow you to mark seam lines, which are important for accurate hand piecing.
- Unless you have special rotary templates, curved shapes are easier to mark and cut with templates.
- You might simply prefer the slower-paced motions of marking and cutting out individual patches.

Machine-piecing templates

Templates used for machine piecing include a 7.5 mm ($\frac{1}{4}$") seam allowance around all sides. The most important line is the cutting line. Position these templates right-side up on the fabric, then mark around them. Shapes can be positioned in a continuous side-by-side arrangement, because seam allowances are included.

Hand-piecing templates

Traditionally, hand-piecing templates do not include a seam allowance. The most important line is the seam line, and experienced hand piecers estimate and add the seam allowance as they cut. If you are a beginner, it's best to mark both the seam and cutting lines – **window templates** make that an easy task (see page 33). Position hand-piecing templates right-side down on the reverse side of fabric, and mark both lines. If you choose to mark only the seam lines, make sure that you leave enough space between shapes to add a 7.5 mm ($\frac{1}{4}$") seam allowance around each one.

Appliqué templates

Templates used for appliqué do not include a seam allowance. There is more about appliqué on pages 69–79.

Making templates

Template plastic is durable, and the best choice for pieces that will be used many times. Several kinds of plastic are available: gridded or plain, transparent or opaque, heat resistant, with two smooth sides or with one rough side that helps grip fabric. Other template options include lightweight cardboard and sandpaper, but the edges of templates made from these materials become distorted with heavy use.

When you make templates, use a fine-tipped pen or pencil to keep marked lines narrow and consistent. Compare each template with the original pattern to make sure it is accurate. Use a fine-tipped marker to mark shapes onto fabric, too.

If you make templates from cardboard or other thick materials, trace the pattern onto paper first, then glue the paper to the template material and cut out. When you use template plastic, it's easy to trace the image from your book directly onto the plastic. Ensure all markings are transferred from the pattern to the template.

What do the marks on pattern pieces mean?

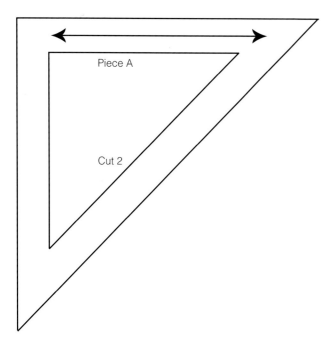

Piece A

Cut 2

■ Transfer all marks to templates

■ Arrows on pattern pieces show you which way the straight grain should flow. Transfer the arrows to your templates, and place them parallel to the straight grain when marking fabric. See Chapter 1 for more information about fabric grain.

■ An 'R' or the word 'Reverse' on a template means that the piece should be turned upside down for some cuts. The reversed patches are mirror images of the original.

■ Small 'ticks' in the seam allowance are registration marks, which help you to align curved edges for sewing.

■ Pattern pieces are usually marked with a set of identifying labels (1, 2, 3, A, B, C, etc.).

Using a light box

A light box is helpful for tracing templates and other motifs. Commercial light boxes are available, but you can make a temporary version by placing a light under any glass-topped table. Turn on the light, then position the original pattern under a sheet of paper. The light will shine through the layers and make the pattern more visible.

Window templates

This versatile kind of template works with most methods. Draw both the seam line and the cutting line on template material, then cut on both lines (a craft knife is helpful for cutting the inner line). The inside of the template falls away, leaving an open window of the shape with the seam allowance surrounding it. Window templates are perfect for hand sewing because they allow you to mark seam and cutting lines in one step. They are a good choice for marking seam intersections on pieces that must be set in (see page 37). They are also handy for targeting specific designs in a printed fabric.

Take window templates along when you shop for fabric, even if you plan to rotary cut patches for a quilt. Place the templates against a print for a preview of how the fabric will look when cut and sewn into patches. Move the template around on the fabric to see if the look is consistent – it could vary quite a bit on large-scale prints. Variations might work just fine for your quilt, but knowing about them in advance means that there won't be any surprises after the fabric is cut and sewn.

Template tips

- Glue sandpaper on the back of templates, rough-side down, to grip fabric. A dab of rubber cement works in the same way. Let it dry thoroughly before using.
- Use a straight edge to guide your marker.
- Use a rotary cutter with an old blade to cut out straight-sided templates.

- Many companies make templates, usually from thick acrylic or metal. If you like the template assembly method, consider building a collection of these long-lasting templates in common shapes and sizes.

- A window template lying on fabric

5

Piecing basics

Machine piecing is great for speedy assembly, but hand piecing is perfect when you need a project you can work on in waiting rooms, on your lunch break, or when you just want to sit and relax. Sometimes you'll find an oddly shaped piece that is much easier to deal with by hand than by machine. When that happens, don't hesitate to mix the two techniques to achieve the perfect block.

Machine piecing

Sewing accurate seams

Before you begin to machine piece, make sure your sewing machine is set up to sew an exact 7.5 mm seam, the metric seam allowance used for quilts. For those working in the Imperial system, instructions for pieced blocks in this book include a $\frac{1}{4}$" seam allowance. You may think a small variation in seams won't matter, but when an error multiplies throughout the quilt, it can keep adjoining units from matching correctly. Unless you use a method such as foundation piecing, accurate seams are a must.

1   Cut three strips of fabric, each exactly 5 cm × 7.5 cm (2" × 3"). Sew the strips together lengthwise with a 7.5 mm ($\frac{1}{4}$") seam allowance. Press the allowances toward the outer strips.

2   Measure the centre strip. It should be exactly 3.5 cm ($1\frac{1}{2}$") wide along its entire length. If its width is different:
   ■   Check that the raw edges did not shift away from each other during assembly.
   ■   If you gauged the distance using a special presser foot, adjust where the fabric moves under the foot. If the strip is too narrow, shorten the allowance by feeding patches through with edges slightly left of the foot's right edge. Shift patches to the right if you must increase the allowance.
   ■   Change the needle position for the next test set.
   ■   If the strip is too narrow, you can sometimes correct the width with a thorough pressing (see page 46).

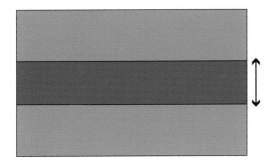

■   Sewing accurate seams

■   Accurate seams in practice

Try a few more test units. If seams are still not accurate, mark a sewing guide directly on the machine's footplate.

1   Position a strip of 7.5 mm graph paper under the presser foot. Drop the needle directly on a line of the paper, leaving one 7.5 mm grid to its right. Lower the presser foot, making sure its edges are parallel to the lines. Align a piece of masking tape with the paper's right edge. If you use Imperial dimensions, do the same, but place the tape $\frac{1}{4}$" from the needle. Use an accurate ruler to draw extra lines on the graph paper as needed.

2 Sew a test set, press, and check strip measurements again. If not accurate, shift the tape to the right or left. Keep testing until you are sewing an accurate 7.5 mm ($\frac{1}{4}$") seam.

3 Once you've established the correct position, apply several more pieces of masking tape over the first to form a better guide for fabric. Other guide options are self-adhesive moleskin and thick strips of adhesive-backed acrylic, available from quiltmaking suppliers.

Scant seams

When you use rotary-cutting techniques, your adjusted seam will probably be what is called a **scant** seam allowance – a little narrower than the stated width. Rotary-cut pieces are often slightly smaller than their template-cut counterparts, because the process of marking and cutting out a template, then marking and cutting out patches, tends to add a little extra width to pieces. When you piece a template-cut quilt, you might need to adjust the seam allowance slightly to compensate for the extra width.

Sewing patches together

Patches are positioned right sides together for sewing. When side-by-side patches have edges of the same

shape the edges should match exactly, but when shapes are different it is sometimes difficult to determine how they align. When matching unlike edges, remember that it's only the seam allowances at their tips that differ; the actual seamlines of each patch will still match. If you are ever in doubt, measure inward 7.5 mm ($\frac{1}{4}$") to mark seam intersections on the reverse side of patches, then pin-match those intersections before sewing.

Assembling a block

Most machine-pieced blocks are assembled by joining individual patches in rows, then sewing the rows together. The two layers of each seam allowance are pressed in one direction, where they create a slight loft on the front side of the quilt. If seams in adjacent units are pressed in opposite directions, the opposing lofts butt together snugly when patches are aligned for sewing, which helps you achieve a perfect match at seam intersections.

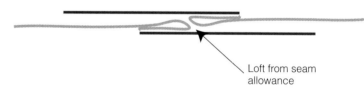

Loft from seam allowance

■ Butt opposing lofts for a perfect match

Did you know?

Strip piecing eliminates the need to cut and sew individual patches. See page 47 for more information.

Chain piecing

To use this time-saving method, feed a matched pair of patches through the machine, but instead of cutting the threads, continue feeding more pairs under the presser foot. When all are sewn, clip threads between paired units and press (see page 37).

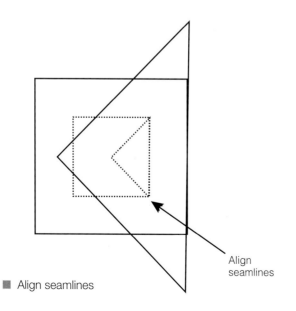

Align seamlines

■ Align seamlines

■ Chain piecing

Setting in

Some blocks can't be assembled by sewing rows together with continuous seams. Instead, pieces must be **set in** to an opening left by previously joined patches. The most important thing to remember about set-in patches is that seams *never* extend into seam allowances. If you mark intersections on patches before beginning, you will find that setting in is an easy task.

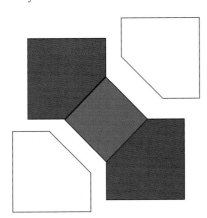

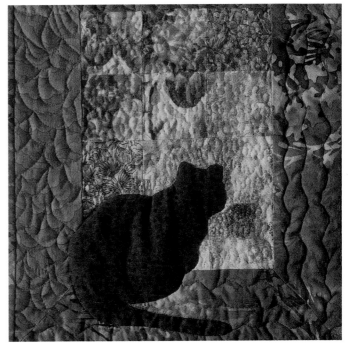

■ Set-in blocks are framed with fabric

Practice setting in by making this traditional Bow-Tie block. Use scraps of three different fabrics: a light, a dark, and a medium.

1 Make window templates (see page 32) of pattern pieces Bow-Tie A and Bow-Tie B on page 118. Mark and cut out one dark A centre, two light B backgrounds, and two dark B Bow-Ties. Place the appropriate template face down on the back of each patch. Use the inner window of the template to mark all seam intersections.

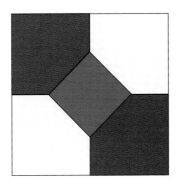

■ Recognising set-in seams

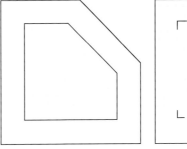
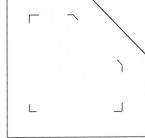

■ Mark all seam intersections

piecing basics

2 Align a dark Bow-Tie patch with one side of the centre square, right sides together. Match seam intersections at ends and secure with pins. Sew a line from one intersection to the other, backstitching at the beginning and end to add stability to the seam. Sew another Bow-Tie patch to the opposite side of the centre square.

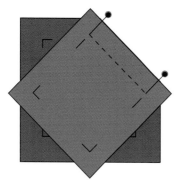

3 Align a light background patch to the centre square, matching seams. Seam intersections of the light patch should be directly over the sewn lines of patches below. Sew the background to the square between intersections, backstitching at the beginning and end.

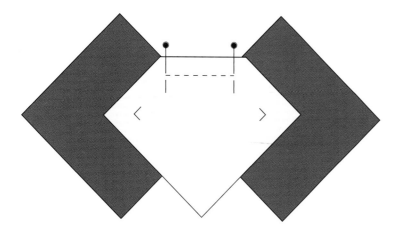

4 Pin an edge of the background to the adjoining edge of a Bow-Tie patch, matching seam intersections where the previous seam ended. Begin sewing at that spot. Backstitch, then continue sewing to the ends of the patches, since the outer edge does not involve set-in pieces. Repeat to attach the opposite side of the

background to the adjoining Bow-Tie patch. Add the background piece to the opposite side in the same way.

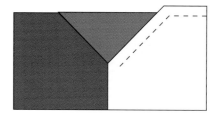

Setting in with rotary-cut patches

The Bow-Tie block was assembled using templates, but it's just as easy to set in using rotary-cut pieces. Make window templates to match the cut size of each shape involved in the setting in process, then use a rotary ruler to measure inward 7.5 mm ($\frac{1}{4}$"). Cut out the inner window, and use the templates to mark seam intersections on the reverse side of patches.

Partial seams

At first glance, the rectangles surrounding the centre of the block shown here appear to be set in but there's an easier way to assemble this block – by sewing partial seams. For this method, a half-seam is sewn first, then remaining units are sewn to each side.

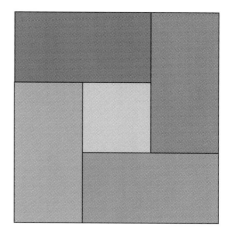

■ Bright Hopes block

Practice partial seams by making a 30 cm (12") Bright Hopes block. Use 7.5 mm ($\frac{1}{4}$") seams throughout.

1 Cut a 11.5 cm (4½") square from light fabric. Cut a 11.5 × 21.5 cm (4½" × 8½") rectangle from each of four different medium fabrics.

2 Align the light centre square with a medium rectangle, right sides together as shown. Begin stitching at the end of the patches and sew until you reach the midpoint of the square. Backstitch and remove from the machine. Press the partial seam towards the centre square.

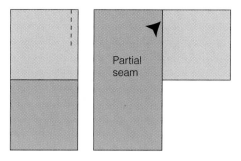

Partial seam

3 Align another rectangle right-side down, placing its long edge across the seamed end of previous patches. It should match the length of the sewn unit. Sew a seam along the entire edge. Press the seam towards the centre square.

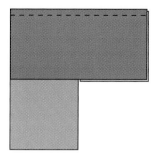

4 Add the third and fourth rectangles in the same way, sewing each one to the entire length of the block.

5 The fourth rectangle creates a straight edge where you can complete the partial seam. Align raw edges along that side and begin stitching where the partial seam ended. Backstitch, then stitch to the end of the block.

Press. Before setting in, analyse similar blocks to see if they can be assembled using partial seams.

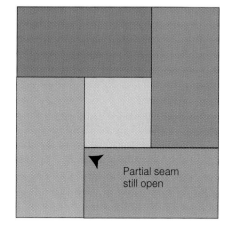

Partial seam still open

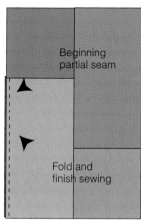

Beginning partial seam

Fold and finish sewing

Curved seams

Most patchwork blocks are arrangements of straight-sided, geometric shapes, but some include curves. Practice piecing curves by making a small Drunkard's Path wallhanging. Make window templates of Drunkard's Path patterns A and B on page 118. Ensure all markings are transferred to the templates. Choose a light, medium and dark fabric, 25 cm (¼ yd) of each.

1 Align templates right-side down on the reverse side of the fabric. Mark and cut eight dark A patches, eight light A patches, eight medium B patches, and eight light B patches. Ensure registration marks are transferred to the seam allowance of each piece.

2 Align a dark A patch with a light B patch, matching registration marks right sides together. Pin at the match.

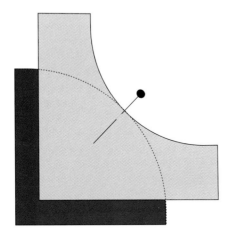

3 Match and pin the end points, then continue matching and pinning along the curved edge. The bias edge should stretch a bit to help you match sides. Sew together with an exact 7.5 mm ($\frac{1}{4}$") seam, placing the flattened quarter circle on the bottom. Press the seam allowance in either direction. Make seven more identical units.

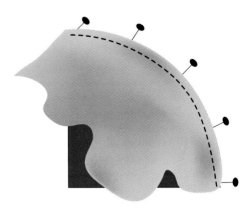

Make tiny clips in the light piece if necessary to help match the edges

4 Make another eight units, with a light A patch and medium B patch. Sew the individual squares together in four rows. Press seams in adjoining rows in opposite directions, then sew rows together. Press and finish edges to make a small wallhanging.

Did you know?

Some quiltmaking supply companies offer rotary-cutting template sets for the Drunkard's Path and other popular curved-seam blocks.

Hand piecing

Thin needles, called **sharps**, are used for hand piecing. Thread the needle with about 50 cm (20") of good quality cotton thread. Grey or medium-beige threads blend easily with most printed fabrics. Before you begin, refer to page 32 for more information about using templates to mark fabric for hand piecing.

Practice your hand-piecing skills by making a 20 cm (8") basket block.

■ Making up a basket block

You'll need a light fabric and a dark fabric, approximately 15 cm ($\frac{1}{8}$ yd) of each.

■ Choose a light fabric and a dark fabric

1 Make window templates for patterns basket-A, B, and C (see page 117). Mark and cut the following: eight dark from A, eight light from A, two light from B, one dark from C, one light from C. Be sure to align the fabric's straight grain parallel with the arrows on templates.

2 Align a dark A triangle with a light A triangle. Stab pins through both patches to match seam ends. Add a few more pins along the length of patches, making sure that the seams are aligned.

3 Remove a pin from one end and insert the needle through the same hole. Some people like to use a knot at the end of the thread. Others prefer to leave a 2.5 cm (1") tail at the beginning, taking a few backstitches to secure the seam.

4 Use a small running stitch to sew the length of the seam. Do not sew past seam intersections. Take a backstitch every 2 cm (¾") or so to add stability. Frequently check the opposite side of the pair often to ensure that stitches also stay on the rear patch's marked seam line.

5 When you reach the end of the seam, stop sewing and backstitch. Make five more identical triangle squares. Open the triangle pairs and trim the nubs from seam ends.

6 Position the triangle squares in three horizontal rows. Place a light A triangle at the ends of rows 2 and 3. Sew the components of each row together, leaving seam allowances free.

Row 1

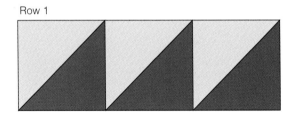

Row 2

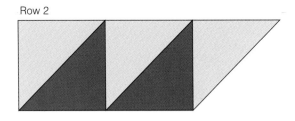

Row 3

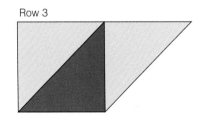

7 Sew rows 1 and 2 together, backstitching when you reach a seam allowance. Insert the needle through the base of the allowance, coming out on the opposite side. Take a stitch, then a backstitch. Sew to the end of the row, leaving all seam allowances free. Check often to be sure that your stitches are on the seamlines of both layers. Add row 3 to the unit in the same way.

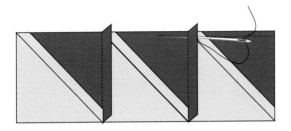

9 Align a light B rectangle to a dark A triangle, right sides together. Sew a seam across the edge, stopping and starting at seam intersections just as you did for triangle squares. Make another B/A unit.

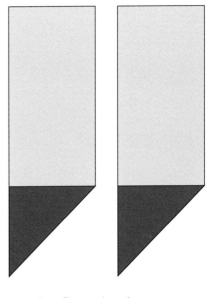

10 Sew one of these B/A units to each side of the larger unit. Finish the block by sewing the light C triangle to the bottom corner of the block. Make more blocks if you wish, then sew together. Press when the quilt top is complete.

8 Fold the dark C triangle in half to find the midpoint of its longest side. Match the midpoint with the midpoint of the unit from step 7. Sew the two together on the seam line.

Even if the instructions for a quilt assume you will piece it by machine, it can be adapted for hand piecing.

- If given, use unfinished patch sizes to make templates, and then mark inward on each side to draw a seam allowance. Trim on both lines to make window templates.
- Sometimes individual patch sizes are not listed, such as for strip-pieced blocks. Use graph paper to draw the finished block to scale. Cut out the pieces and glue them to template material, or trace them onto template plastic. Mark around templates, then use a rotary ruler to add seam allowances around each piece.

English paper piecing

You might hear quilters use the term 'paper piecing' when they talk about piecing on foundations but true English paper piecing is a very different technique. For this method, paper templates are cut for each piece in a quilt, then fabric edges are folded over and basted to the papers. Patches are then sewn together with a **whipstitch**. The papers remain in place until all adjoining patches are sewn, so everything fits together perfectly.

Practice English paper piecing by making the traditional Grandmother's Flower Garden block. Use scraps of four different fabrics: dark, medium, medium-light, and light. The instructions here are traditional, using a template to mark and cut paper foundations and fabric. To speed up the process, use rotary-cutting techniques for both, cutting papers to the finished size of the hexagon, and adding a seam allowance for fabric patches. Refer to page 29 for quick-cut hexagon instructions. Use any hexagon size you want.

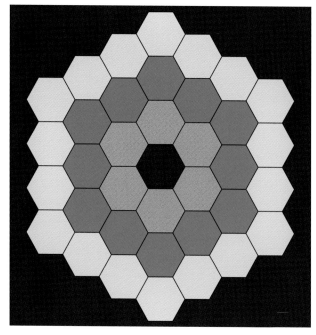

■ Grandmother's Flower Garden Block

1   Make a rigid window template of the hexagon-A pattern on page 121. Make 37 paper templates the size of the inner window. Use a lightweight card that is more sturdy than bond paper but thinner than cardboard. Such card is available from office or art supply shops.

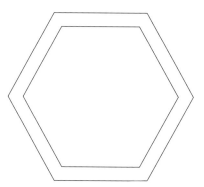

2   Use the outer edge of the rigid hexagon template to mark and cut the following fabric patches: one dark, six medium-light, twelve medium, eighteen light.

3 Centre a template on the reverse of a fabric hexagon and pin to hold. Fold the seam allowances over the paper and baste in place with long stitches. Baste all remaining patches to papers.

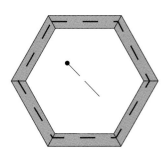

4 Thread a thin needle with one strand of quilting thread, knotted at the end. Align the dark patch with a medium-light patch, right sides together. Hold the patches in place with your fingers. Insert the needle through the folds of the matched edges, barely catching the fabric. Pull the needle through and insert it again from the same direction and very close to the first stitch. Keep stitching to complete the seam. Pull gently after each stitch – hard tugs will distort the patches. Try to avoid sewing through papers.

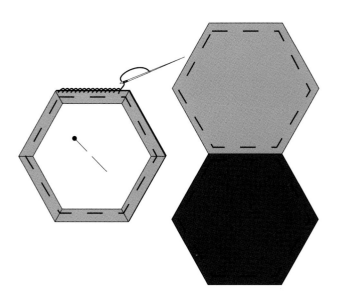

5 Add another medium-light patch to the next side of the dark patch. Continue to surround the dark patch with medium-light patches. Fold the medium-light patches right sides together and sew them together in the same way, knotting or backstitching at the beginning and end of each seam.

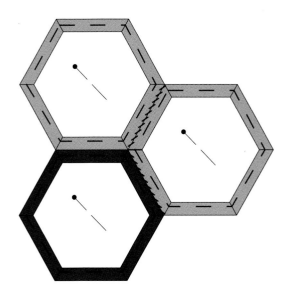

6 Surround the unit with medium hexagons, and then add the light hexagons. Papers and basting stitches can be removed as the centre pieces become completely surrounded by other hexagons.

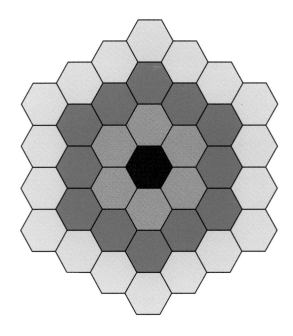

7   Carefully remove papers, and press the outermost seam allowances under. Appliqué the block to a larger background. If you prefer, leave the papers on the block's outer perimeter in place, since edges are already basted under. Appliqué the block to a larger background, taking care to avoid sewing through the papers. When finished, use sharp pointed scissors to trim away the background approximately 1.25 cm (½") inside the line of applique stitches. Remove papers.

8   Alternatively, make a finished size template of the portion of the template required to fill in the zigzag gaps around the edges of the block. Mark and cut 18 dark patches, adding a seam allowance around each. Baste to papers. Sew the partial hexagons to the outer edges of the block. Remove papers, sandwich, quilt and bind as for any small quilt.

9   The single block makes a nice wallhanging. To make a larger piece, sew multiple blocks together, or continue adding rows of hexagons to the original block.

■ Grandmother's Flower Garden block – step 8

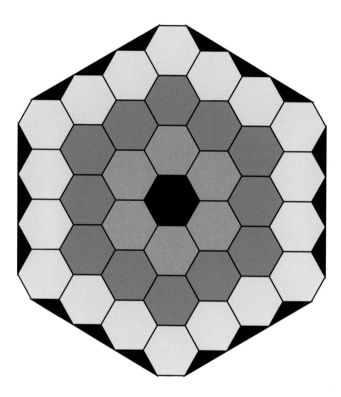

Pressing basics

The most important thing to remember when using an iron on quilts is the word **press**. That is exactly what you must do – press, setting the iron up and down on blocks, letting its heat and weight do the work for you. Moving the iron back and forth across patchwork will stretch it out of shape.

Some quilters like to use steam to press their blocks. If you choose to do that, keep in mind that moisture makes stretch more likely. I prefer to press with a dry iron, keeping a spritzer bottle of water handy for those times when moisture is required to make a seam lie flat.

When you machine piece, press seams in rows before rows are sewn together. Press adjoining seams in opposite directions when possible. Careful, thorough pressing is one way to ensure machine-pieced blocks are accurate. It might seem like a lot more work to keep jumping up to the ironing board, but you'll be surprised how much it improves your piecework. Hand-pieced quilts needn't be pressed until the entire quilt is assembled.

Did you know?

Before you press a seam to one side, set the iron down on it flat, just as it was sewn. This simple step 'sets' the seam, flattening puckers and pulls that may have occurred when sewn.

6

Quick piecing

Quick-piecing methods speed up assembly time and increase accuracy. Instead of cutting individual pieces for each block, sections of blocks are sewn together as larger, multi-patch units, then cut apart. Quick-piecing methods are especially handy for quilts that require large numbers of identical pieces, but they can be easily adapted for scrappy quilts, too.

Strip piecing

For this technique, strips of fabric are sewn together into a long **strip set**, which is configured to look like a portion of the block. Shorter, identical **segments** are cut from the set to replace some of the block's side-by-side patches.

■ Strip pieced segments

Practice strip piecing skills by making a Single Irish Chain wallhanging. Five-pieced blocks are sewn together with plain alternate squares between them. The design in the pieced blocks links at corners to form an attractive diagonal pattern. You'll need 30 cm

($\frac{1}{3}$ yd) of a dark fabric, 1.2 m ($1\frac{1}{4}$ yd) of a medium-dark fabric, and 70 cm ($\frac{3}{4}$ yd) of a light fabric. Before you begin, practice your rotary skills, and read page 35 to make sure you are sewing an exact 7.5 mm ($\frac{1}{4}$") seam allowance. The finished block size is 30 cm (12").

■ Irish chain wallhanging

1   Rotary cut the following:
   four 6.5 cm × 70 cm dark strips ($2\frac{1}{2}$" × 27")
   one 11.5 cm × 62 cm medium-dark strip ($4\frac{1}{2}$" × 25")
   one 11.5 cm × 70 cm light strip ($4\frac{1}{2}$" × 27")
   two 6.5 cm × 62 cm light strips ($2\frac{1}{2}$" × 25")
   one 21.5 cm × 70 cm light strip ($8\frac{1}{2}$" × 27")
   ten 6.5 cm × 21.5 cm light strips ($2\frac{1}{2}$" × $8\frac{1}{2}$")
   four 31.5 cm × 31.5 cm medium-dark squares
   ($12\frac{1}{2}$" × $12\frac{1}{2}$")

2   Sew a 6.5 cm × 62 cm ($2\frac{1}{2}$" × 25") light strip to each side of the 11.5 cm × 62 cm ($4\frac{1}{2}$" × 25") medium-dark strip. Press seam allowances towards the dark strip.

3 Square up one end of the strip set, using the same technique you used to square up the edge of fabric. Cut five 11.5 cm (4½") long segments from the strip set, taking care to keep its leading edge at 90° to its bottom edge. Set aside.

4 Sew a 6.5 cm × 70 cm (2½" × 27") dark strip to each side of the 11.5 cm × 70 cm (4½" × 27") light strip. Press seam allowances towards the dark strips. Square up one end of the strip set and cut ten 6.5 cm (2½") long segments from it. Set aside.

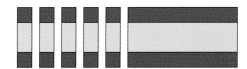

5 Sew a 6.5 cm × 70 cm (2½" × 27") dark strip to each side of the 21.5 cm × 70 cm (8½" × 27") light strip. Press seam allowances towards the dark strips. Square up one end and cut ten 6.5 cm (2½") long segments from it. Set aside.

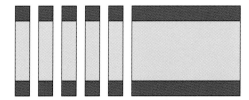

6 Matching seam intersections carefully, sew a segment from step 4 to the top and bottom of a segment from step 3. Press seam allowances towards the block's centre.

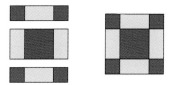

7 Sew a 6.5 cm × 21.5 cm (2½" × 8½") light bar to each side of the new unit. Press seam allowances towards the centre of the block.

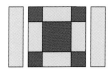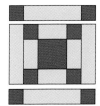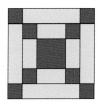

8 Sew a step 5 segment to the top and bottom of the block. Press seam allowances towards the centre of the block. Repeat all steps to make four more Single Irish Chain blocks.

9 Arrange the blocks in three horizontal rows of three blocks each, alternating pieced blocks with the 31.5 cm (12½") medium-dark squares. Sew components of each row together, pressing seam allowances towards the alternate blocks. Join rows, matching the seams carefully. Once finished you can either add a border (see Chapter 10), or quilt and bind the wallhanging as it is. The alternate blocks are a good place to practice your hand-quilting skills.

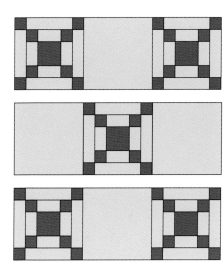

Strip-piecing tips

- Press strips together before sewing, to help them adhere to each other. Use fine silk pins to hold edges together if necessary.
- Press after adding each strip. Place the strip set on your ironing board with the strip the seam allowance will be pressed towards on top. Press the seam flat, just as it was sewn. Open the unit with your fingers and press the iron into the seam gently. Use an up-and-down motion – *do not* drag the iron back and forth.
- Work with shorter strips until you are more comfortable with the technique. To determine strip length, multiply the cut size of segments by the number of segments you wish to cut. Add approximately 5 cm (2") to this length to allow for squaring up.
- Use shorter strips from a variety of fabrics to make a scrappy quilt.

■ Strip pieced quilt

Quick-pieced half-square triangle units

Half-square triangle units are made by sewing together two right triangles along their long, diagonal edges. Each triangle occupies one half of the resulting square. This versatile square, also called a **triangle square**, is one of the most commonly used patchwork units.

■ Triangle square

When you are hand piecing, or working with small bits of fabric, you might prefer to make triangle squares by cutting and sewing together individual triangles in the traditional manner. But when you wish to speed up the process – and enhance accuracy – consider using a quick-piecing method to make them. Both of the methods described in this chapter eliminate the need to cut individual triangles, which means you won't have to handle stretchy, bias edges.

Method 1: matched squares

Squares of fabric are sewn together to the left and right of the diagonal, then cut apart and pressed open to form triangle squares. Each pair of squares yields two pieced triangle square units. This is a good method to use when you are making a scrappy quilt, or when you have lots of small pieces of fabric to work with.

1   Add 2.5 cm ($\frac{7}{8}$") to the finished size of a half-square triangle unit. Use that dimension to cut a square from two contrasting fabrics.

2   Use a pencil or permanent marker to draw a diagonal line from corner to corner on the reverse side of the lightest square.

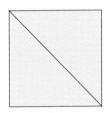

3   Align the edges of both squares, right sides together. Sew a seam 7.5 mm ($\frac{1}{4}$") from both sides of the marked centre line. If your presser foot cannot accurately gauge the distance, mark seams before sewing.

4   Cut through both layers along the centre line. Open the units, pressing seam allowances toward the dark half, or as directed in the pattern. Trim nubs at seam ends. The pieced squares should be exactly 1.5 cm ($\frac{1}{2}$") longer and wider than their finished size. Repeat to make additional triangle squares.

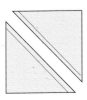 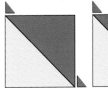

Sew and trim method

Start with squares that are 5 mm ($\frac{1}{4}$") larger than necessary. After sewing, use a square rotary ruler to help you trim back the triangle squares to the exact unfinished size. Choose a ruler with a diagonal line, and position it along the centre seam to make sure squares are trimmed so that each triangle occupies one-half of the square. This method does require an extra step, but yields very accurate units to use in your quilt.

■ Sew and trim method

Method 2: triangle squares on a grid

Sewing on a grid is a good choice when you need many identical units. Each square in the grid produces two triangle square units.

1   To calculate square size, add 2.5 cm ($\frac{7}{8}$") to the finished size of a triangle square unit.
2   To determine how many squares to draw, divide the number of triangle squares required by two.

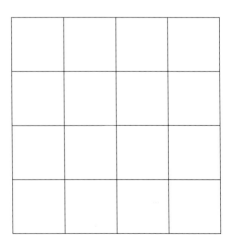

3   Draw the grid on paper, leaving a margin of approximately 1.5 cm ($\frac{1}{2}$") around its outer edges. Tracing paper and newspaper are good choices, because they pull away easily after sewing is complete. Freezer paper is another option.

Did you know?

You can draw the grid directly on the reverse side of your lightest fabric. Press the fabric first, spraying on a bit of starch to stiffen it slightly. Mark with a pencil or permanent marker that glides easily across the woven surface.

4   Draw a diagonal line from corner to corner through each square in the grid.

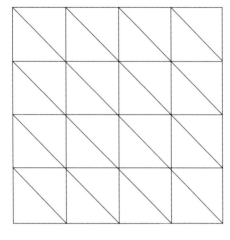

5   Cut two fabrics the same size as the grid. Align fabrics right sides together, pressing to help them adhere to each other. Centre the grid on top of the fabrics and pin it securely through both layers. (Press freezer paper grids to the top layer.)
6   Sew a line exactly 7.5 mm ($\frac{1}{4}$") from each side of the diagonal lines. If your presser foot cannot accurately gauge the distance, draw seam lines on the grid before sewing.
7   Cut triangle squares apart along the grid lines and along the centre diagonals.

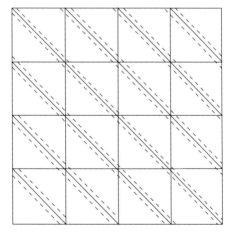

Remove paper and any stitches that might have overlapped into neighbouring units. Press open as in Method 1, trimming away nubs at seam ends. Units should be 1.5 cm ($\frac{1}{2}$") longer and wider than their finished size.

■ Small quilt made with triangle squares

1 Determine the finished size of the quarter-square triangle unit and add 3.5 cm (1¼"). Cut one square from each of two contrasting fabrics.

2 Use half-square triangle Method 1 to assemble two half-square triangle units. Each completed unit should be exactly 2.5 cm (⅞") larger than the finished size of the quarter-square triangle unit.

3 Draw a diagonal line from corner to corner on the reverse side of one triangle square, perpendicular to the seam. Place squares together, dark halves facing lighter halves. Align all edges. Use your fingers to make sure the seams fit snugly into each other.

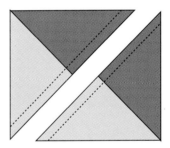

4 Sew a seam 7.5 mm (¼") from each side of the diagonal line, in the same manner as for parent units. Cut apart on the diagonal line. Press units open and trim nubs at the ends of the seam allowance.

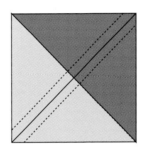

Make scrappy quarter-square units by using a variety of fabrics.

For a slightly different look, pair a half-square triangle with a square of plain fabric to make two mirror-image pieced units.

Quick-pieced quarter-square triangle units

These popular units look difficult, but they are easy to quick piece when you use oversized half-square triangle units as their 'parents'.

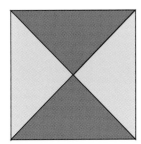

■ Quarter-square triangle units

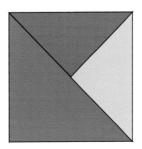
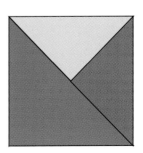

■ Mirror-image pieced units

7

Foundation piecing

F oundation piecing is a fast and fun technique that lets you ignore the rules about precise cutting and sewing. If you can sew on a straight line, you can make a perfect foundation-pieced block every time. Watch out though, this technique can be addictive!

Foundation piecing is a traditional method which eliminates the need for perfectly cut patches and precise seam allowances. Patches are cut to approximate sizes, and sewn onto a foundation, a base made from fabric, paper, or other materials. For the first method in this chapter, an exact replica of a block is drawn on each foundation and seams are sewn directly on the marked lines.

Foundation piecing is possible if a patch can be sewn to the entire side of another patch or group of patches, such as in the traditional Log Cabin block (see page 55). Piecing begins in the centre of the block, and continues outward in numerical order. Each new log is stitched across the entire length or width of earlier logs. If it sounds confusing, don't worry. After you make a few practice blocks you'll be ready to tackle any foundation project.

Did you know?

The foundation method is sometimes called 'Flip and Sew', 'Sew and Flip', and 'Paper Piecing'.

■ Crazy quilt in progress

Selecting a foundation material

Foundations can be permanent or temporary: permanent foundations remain in the quilt forever, temporary foundations are removed from blocks after they are all sewn together, but before the quilt is sandwiched with batting and backing. There are advantages and disadvantages to each type of foundation, so choose one that is appropriate for your project.

Permanent versus temporary foundations

- Permanent foundations add an extra layer. That isn't a problem if you intend to machine quilt, but it makes hand quilting more difficult, especially where seam allowances add even more bulk.
- Permanent foundations allow you to use odd-sized scraps of fabric without consideration for where stretchy bias edges are placed. The foundation will always be there to stabilise patches.
- Short, sturdy stitches are used with temporary foundations, so that seams stay intact when foundations are pulled away. Stitch length can be slightly longer with permanent foundations, making it easier to correct an error.
- It takes time to remove temporary foundations.

It sounds as if I prefer permanent foundations, doesn't it? But even though it takes a little more time, I nearly always use temporary foundations for blocks that will be sewn into a quilt, because I do not like the bulk of an extra layer. When I'm making blocks for other reasons – to decorate clothing, or for Christmas ornaments, for example – the increased stiffness is often helpful. It's a matter of personal choice, so experiment with all kinds of foundations to see which types work best for you in different situations.

■ Log Cabin quilt

Permanent foundation materials

Prewashed, **lightweight muslin** is one choice for permanent foundations. It is a woven cloth, and so has a tendency to stretch with handling, which can result in skewed blocks. Moisture makes stretch more likely, so use a dry iron to press muslin-backed blocks during assembly. Coating muslin foundations with a little spray starch helps keep stretch to a minimum.

Non-woven interfacing is a less bulky choice for permanent foundations. It doesn't stretch, and foundation lines are visible from both sides.

Temporary foundation materials

Vellum and **smooth tracing paper** are good choices for temporary foundations. Both remain stable as the block is assembled, but tear away easily when sewing is complete. Marked lines are visible from both sides, which leads to faster and more accurate patch placement. Fabrics stick to tracing paper when pressed, which helps keep already-sewn patches in place as new patches are added. Vellum and smooth tracing paper will feed through most desktop printers.

Plain newsprint is available in pads at office and art supply shops. It is easier to remove than heavier bond papers. Newsprint will feed through most desktop printers.

Tissue paper is easy to remove but sometimes tears away before you want it to. Reserve it for blocks with just a few pieces, where handling is minimal. Tissue paper is too delicate to feed through printers.

Easy tear is a non-woven material that resembles interfacing, but is stiffer. It remains stable as you assemble blocks and is easy to remove when sewing is complete. Although it is not available in all areas, you can order it from quilting supply catalogues.

Making the foundations

Foundations are sewing blueprints, and accuracy in constructing them is essential. Each finished block is an image of its foundation, so if the foundations aren't accurate the blocks won't be either. No matter which method you choose to make foundations, compare all copies to make sure that they are an exact match.

- Trace each image individually, using a light box if necessary (see page 32). Choose mechanical pencils or fine-tipped permanent markers to draw thin, accurate lines. Use a straight edge to guide your pen so that lines match the pattern exactly.
- Trace the image onto paper with a hot iron transfer pen, then use the master to transfer the drawing to the foundations. Baking parchment is a good material for the master image, because it can withstand the high temperatures of repeated

ironing. When the image no longer transfers, draw over the lines again with the pen.

- Trace the image onto a sheet of paper. Stack four or five sheets of foundation paper under the drawing and hold the stack in place with staples. Machine-sew through all marked lines with an unthreaded needle. Punched holes should form easy-to-follow lines, but should not be so close together that foundations fall apart during assembly. The raised edges on the reverse side of punched lines will grip the fabric, which helps to keep pieces from shifting as you sew.
- Stack foundation material, alternating it with dressmaker's carbon paper. Place the original on top and secure the layers. Roll a seamstress's tracing wheel along the lines of the original. Thin materials such as tracing paper and non-woven interfacing are good choices for this transfer method.
- If you are careful, you can use photocopies. Choose a high-quality copier, and set it to reproduce at exactly 100%. Place the pattern near the centre of the copier's image area, flat against the glass. Always copy the original pattern, because copies of copies are more likely to be distorted.
- Use a computer drawing program to reproduce patterns, or scan them at 100%. Print the images onto paper. Press with a dry iron during block assembly, especially with ink jet foundations, because steam is likely to make the inks bleed. Place a piece of muslin on top of your ironing board before pressing blocks so that residue from ink or toner will end up on the muslin, not your ironing board cover.
- Look for pre-printed foundations, both temporary and permanent. Rubber stamps of blocks are available too – simply press the stamp onto an ink pad then transfer the image to a foundation. Stencils are another choice, and are available for many traditional quilt blocks. As long as foundation piecing remains popular with quilters, you can be sure new products will be introduced.

Transferring markings

Transfer all the markings on the original pattern to each foundation. Before you begin sewing, you'll find it helpful to write a few short reminders on your foundations, such as 'dark fabric' or 'light fabric'. Pre-marking foundations speeds up assembly, especially when you are working with intricate or non-symmetrical blocks.

Stitch length

Stitches should be shorter than normal, but the ideal length depends on the project and the type of foundation material used. For instance, very short seams in miniature blocks require a short stitch length to keep them from unravelling when temporary foundations are removed. Between 5.5 and 8 stitches per centimetre (14 and 20 stitches per inch) is the normal range.

Straight grain position

Stretch is minimised when edges on the perimeter of a block are cut on the straight grain. Even though odd-sized scraps can be used for foundation piecing, try to position patches so that the grain is aligned correctly.

Needle and thread

Begin each project with a new needle. The needle must pierce multiple layers of foundations and fabric, so it becomes dull quite quickly. Larger needles help punch out paper foundations for easier removal, but they are usually not the best choice for your quilt. Choose needle and thread sizes by determining how the two must work together.

Did you know?

Old machine needles that are too dull to use on fabric are great for punch-marking paper foundations.

Foundation piece a Log Cabin block

The best way to learn foundation piecing is to make a block. The traditional Log Cabin block is assembled with a scrappy assortment of light fabrics on one side of the diagonal, and darker fabrics on the other. The fabrics on same sides should be of similar values, but there should be a definite contrast in value between the two sides. Read more about value on page 9.

Did you know?

The centre of antique Log Cabin blocks is often red, a colour chosen to represent the 'heart' of the cabin.

1   Make a foundation of the Log Cabin pattern on page 116. Leave a little excess foundation material extending past the outermost lines of the image. Transfer all log numbers to the foundation. Mark the light and dark sides of the block.

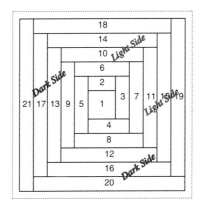

2   Cut a 3.8 cm (1½") square for the centre log.
3   Cut a 2.5 cm (1") wide strip from several dark and light fabrics. Strips at least 18 cm (7") long will allow you to use any fabric in any position, but shorter strips will work for shorter logs.

4   Position the centre square right-side up on the reverse (unprinted) side of the foundation, centring it over the area for log 1. Secure it with a dab of glue. Hold the foundation up to the light, printed side facing you. You should be able to see a shadow of the fabric square. Do its edges overlap the outer lines of log 1 fairly evenly? If not, reposition the square and check again.

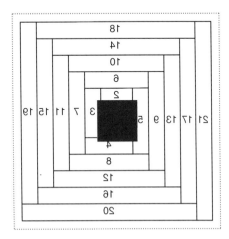

Did you know?

The first piece of each block is the only one positioned right-side up. All remaining pieces are positioned right-side down for sewing.

5   Select a light fabric for log 2. Place the strip right-side down on top of log 1, matching the upper and left edges of both pieces. Trim the right edge of the strip flush with the right edge of log 1.

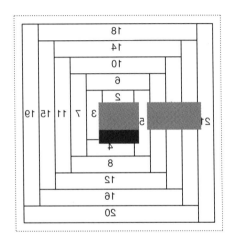

6   Holding the fabrics in place, turn the foundation over. Sew a seam on the line separating log 1 from log 2, beginning and ending the seam 3–5 stitches on each side of the line. (If you find it difficult to judge the starting point, extend the drawn lines a bit with a sharp pencil.)

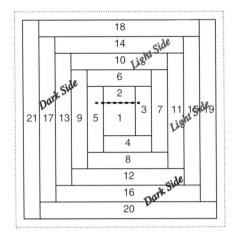

7   Remove the block from the machine. Turn to the reverse side of the foundation and check to make sure the seam allowance is adequate – it should be 0.5–0.6 cm ($\frac{3}{16}$"–$\frac{1}{4}$") wide. Flip log 2 to a right-side up position and finger press in place.

8   Hold the foundation up to the light, printed side facing you. Does the shadow of log 2 overlap all unsewn lines around its edges? Is the overlap enough to create a stable seam allowance on each side when those seams are sewn? If so, press log 2 right-side up.

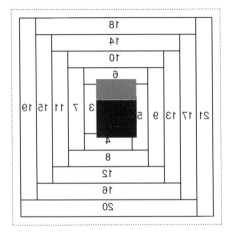

9 Choose another light fabric for log 3. Position the strip right-side down, aligning its top edge with the top edge of log 2, and its left edge with the left edges of logs 1 and 2. Don't worry if the edges of logs 1 and 2 aren't exactly even. Trim away the excess length of the strip, leaving the new edge flush with the bottom of log 1.

10 Holding the fabrics in place, turn to the printed side of the foundation. Sew a seam on the line that separates logs 1 and 2 from log 3, beginning and ending it four or five stitches on either side of the line.

11 Flip log 3 right-side up. Check to make sure its edges extend past all unsewn lines that border its shape. Trim the new seam allowance to an even width and press log 3 in place.

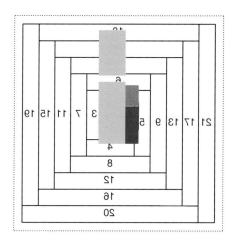

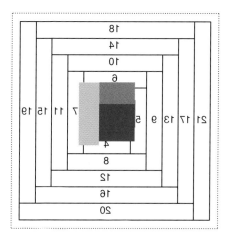

12 Log 4 is added in the same way. Choose a dark strip and position it right-side down along the lower edges of logs 3 and 1. Trim the strip flush with the right-hand edge of log 1. Turn the foundation over and sew on the line separating logs 1 and 3 from log 4, beginning and ending the seam slightly past the line.

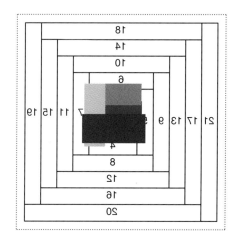

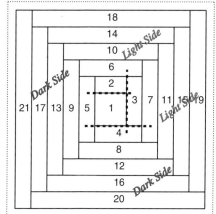

13 Remove the block from the machine and check placement of the new log. Trim the seam, then flip the log right-side up and press in place.

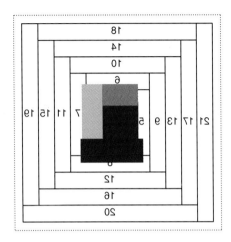

15 The remaining logs are added in exactly the same way, moving in a circular motion around the centre of the block. When complete, the edges of the outer logs should extend slightly past the perimeter of the foundation, represented by a dashed line on the original pattern.

16 Press the finished block. Using scissors or rotary-cutting equipment, trim through all layers on the outermost line. This final step creates an exact 7.5 mm ($\frac{1}{4}$") seam allowance around the block. Make additional blocks if you like, leaving temporary foundations in place until blocks are sewn together. See page 55 to get an idea of how your finished quilt should look.

14 Choose another dark strip for log 5. Position it right-side down along the right-hand edges of logs 1, 2 and 4. Trim excess length if necessary. Flip the unit over and sew on the line that separates logs 1, 2 and 4 from log 5. Check placement and trim seam as for other logs. Flip log 5 right-side up and press in place.

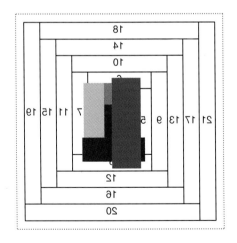
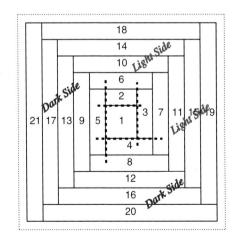
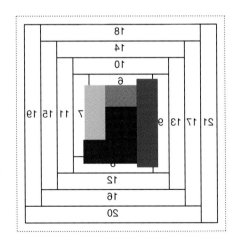

Blocks are mirror images of the foundation

Because patches are sewn to the reverse side of foundations, the finished blocks are a mirror image of the printed side. To sew mirror images of the same pattern, make your foundations from vellum or another sheer material, so that lines are visible from both sides. Assemble an original block by sewing on the reverse side of a foundation, and its mirror image by sewing on the front side of a foundation. Use markers you're sure won't bleed when you sew on top of marked lines.

Segment piecing

Sometimes it is not possible to foundation piece a block as one unit, but the accuracy that can be achieved using foundations is good motivation to piece the block in segments. The block shown here is foundation pieced in three segments, and then the segments are sewn together to complete the block. As you become more accustomed to the simplicity of foundation piecing, you will discover many ways to use the technique.

Foundation piecing tips

Here are a few other things to remember as you foundation piece.

- Trim the seam allowance to an even width after sewing each seam, otherwise you will end up with a thick mass of extra fabric on the back of the block.
- If you find it's difficult to judge patch placement, use slightly wider strips of fabric. Your accuracy will improve once you are more familiar with the technique, allowing you to switch to narrower strips again.
- Don't worry if the raw edges of patches don't exactly match. It's important to have enough of an overlap for stable seam allowances, but edges are evened up as seams are trimmed.
- Keep a pair of tweezers handy for removing little bits of temporary foundations. A blunt-tipped tapestry needle will help you remove bits of paper from under stitches.
- Have fun – this should be a stress-free technique! Patch sizes given with foundation projects are approximate. If you have slightly larger scraps, don't bother to cut them to recommended sizes. Make use of smaller patches by using less of an overlap, which narrows the seam allowance.
- If this method is new to you, determine patch dimensions by adding 9 mm ($\frac{3}{8}$") seam allowance around all sides of a finished shape. After a little practice, you can reduce patch sizes to include a 7.5 mm ($\frac{1}{4}$") seam allowance.

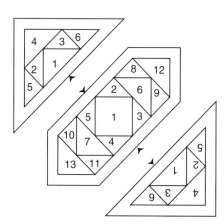

■ Segment piecing

Crazy quilts

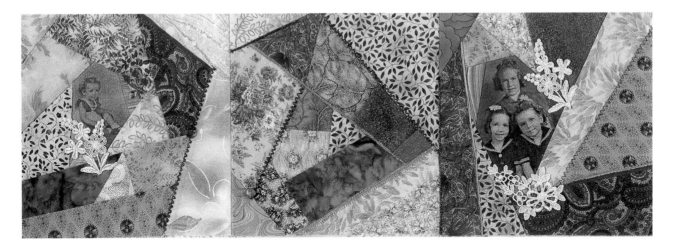

Crazy quilt patches are sewn onto a plain, unmarked foundation. As there are no lines to follow the design is random, with the final shape of individual pieces determined by how you cut them, and where you decide to sew seams.

Crazy quilts became popular during the late 1800s. Most were used as decorative throws, rather than bed quilts. Those who could afford it added velvets, silks, and satins, while quilters of more moderate means used mostly cottons and wools, scattering just a few special fabrics throughout the design. Printed silks were a favourite addition, and were readily available in the form of souvenir ribbons and cigar and cigarette wrappers.

After the quilt top was assembled, the quiltmaker added all kinds of embellishments, including laces, hand embroidery, charms, buttons, beads, and silk flowers. Doilies and fancy handkerchiefs were incorporated into the design too, sometimes becoming the backdrop for embroidery. Names and important dates were often included in the design.

Today's quilters have an endless selection of fabrics to choose from. We can mimic the look of a vintage quilt, or make it with colour-splashed contemporary prints. We can adorn our quilts with hand embroidery, or finish them more quickly with decorative machine stitching.

We can even add photographs by feeding fabric or photo-transfer paper through a desktop printer. Your crazy quilt will be a lasting memento if you make it a reflection of special times from your own life.

Making a crazy quilt

Crazy quilts can be pieced on any size foundation, but sewing together individual blocks makes a project more manageable.

- Most crazy quilts are pieced on permanent foundations. Use non-woven interfacing, or try prewashed muslin for a firmer base.
- Cut foundations 2.5 cm (1") longer and wider than the finished size of the block. The larger size compensates for distortion that sometimes occurs during assembly. It also gives you more flexibility later if you choose to overlap patches to camouflage seams.
- Increase the quilt's visual texture by selecting a good assortment of print scales and types, including florals, geometrics, pictorials, stripes, plaids, solids, and tone-on-tone prints. Choose fabrics of different colour value, so that some patches will contrast with each other.

Piecing from the centre

1 Cut a small piece of fabric
with three, five or seven
edges. Pin it right-side up,
near the block's centre.
Avoid placing it directly on
the centre point.

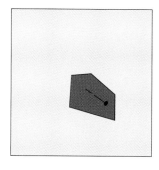

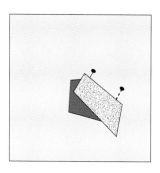

2 Lay another piece of
fabric right-side down
along one edge of the
first. Mark the endpoints
of the first piece with
straight pins if the ends
of the second fabric
extend past them. Sew a
7.5 mm ($\frac{1}{4}$") wide seam
between the pins.

3 Flip the new piece right-
side up and press it in
place. Trim the edges of
the new piece to align
with the edges of the
first.

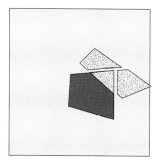

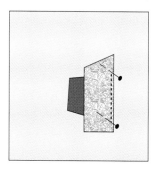

4 Working in a clockwise
direction, align another
piece of fabric right-side
down along the next
angle of the centre patch.
The new piece should
also extend across the
width of the second
patch. Sew a seam
7.5 mm ($\frac{1}{4}$") from the

edge, marking underneath endpoints with a pin if
necessary. Flip piece 3 right-side up and press it in place.
Trim if necessary.

5 Add piece 4 in the same way, aligning it with the next
angle of the centre patch, and making sure it extends
across all previous patches. Work clockwise to sew
remaining pieces to the centre patch, then continue
outward in a circular motion, covering the outer patches,
until the foundation is filled.

6 Trim through all layers, squaring up the block to the
correct unfinished size. Repeat to make as many blocks
as your project requires.

Camouflaging seams

It's easy to camouflage seams where blocks are sewn
together. Before you square up a block, fold back the
ends of a few outer patches, leaving their lengths
intact. Keep the patches folded back while you sew
the partially trimmed edge to a block with a fully
trimmed edge. Fold the patches across the seam, onto
the second block. Turn the edges under and appliqué
in place.

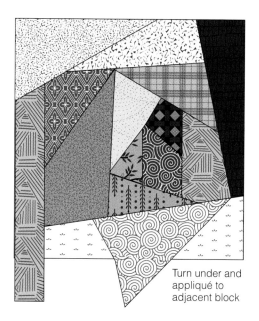

Turn under and
appliqué to
adjacent block

■ Camouflaging seams

Hiding long seams

There may be times you wish to break up a long seam line. Sew smaller pieces of fabric together to form a strip, then sew the strip to the foundation as one unit. Use different shapes and seam angles for best results.

■ Hiding seams

Adding curves

Cut a curved patch with a straight edge along one side. Sew the straight edge to the foundation, then flip the patch right-side up. Mark the curve on the foundation below, then flip the piece back out of the way again.

Sew straight edge

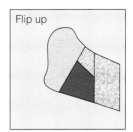
Flip up

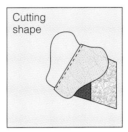
Cutting shape

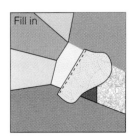
Fill in

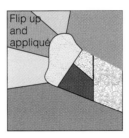
Flip up and appliqué

■ Adding curves

Add more pieces to the foundation, their raw edges extending inside the marked line. When all pieces are filled in, turn the patch right-side up again and appliqué it in place to cover the edges of the other patches.

Piecing from a corner

Start piecing from a corner of the foundation, rather than the centre. Work clockwise across the edges of the first patch, then anti-clockwise to sew the next row. Keep adding patches in the same back and forth manner.

Finishing up

Add embroidery and other embellishments after the blocks are sewn together. Finish up with backing and batting as for any other quilt. For a traditional look, choose a thin batting – or none at all. Most traditional crazy quilts were tied, rather than quilted, but the choice is yours.

String piecing

This method is a wonderful way to use leftover scraps from other projects. Strips of fabric – called **strings** – are sewn side-by-side onto an unmarked foundation, with no attempt to 'match' fabrics. Incorporate a variety of colour values, so that strings will contrast with each other. To make a practice block, cut a 22.5 cm (9") foundation. For best results, press after adding each string.

1 Cut several strings of fabric, each approximately 23.75 cm (9½") long, varying their widths from slightly under 2.5 cm (1") to about 5 cm (2"). Pin a string right-side up near the centre of the block. Its ends should extend past the edges of the foundation.

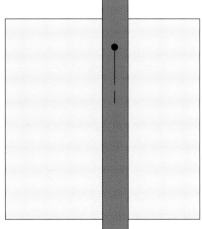

2 Place another string right-side down on top of the first, aligning raw edges on one side. Sew a seam 7.5 cm ($\frac{1}{4}$") from the edge.

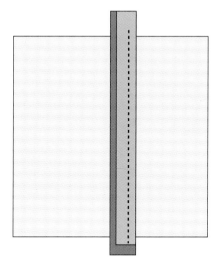

3 Press the second strip right-side up. Add strings to both sides of the first until the foundation is covered. Try to vary the widths of adjacent strings.

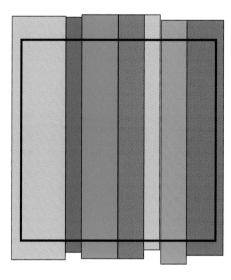

4 Press the block, then square it up, trimming away the string edges that overlap the foundation. Make as many blocks as you need for your project.

Variations

- Cut angles in some of the strings before sewing them to the foundation.
- Cut longer strings, then sew them to the block at an angle. To stabilise bias edges, sew a line of basting stitches just inside the perimeter of the completed block.

- Change string directions. Mark the foundation into two or three sections. Sew strips perpendicular to the lines, with ends overlapping lines slightly. When that area is filled, add the strips parallel to the marked lines.

- Use foundations of any shape: any patch used in quilting can be string pieced.
- Combine string-pieced shapes with plain shapes.
- Use long strips on a large foundation to make a piece of string fabric, then cut several blocks from it.

■ Foundation pieced miniature doll's-house quilt

Appliqué

Appliqué is the process of sewing one or more smaller pieces of fabric onto a larger background. Beginners are sometimes reluctant to try appliqué, because it has the reputation of being 'difficult'. Appliqué does take practice, but is really no harder than sewing together a patchwork block. There are many ways to make an appliqué quilt, so there's sure to be one that's perfect for you.

Appliqué tools

- **Scissors:** a pair of small, sharp scissors that cut all the way to their tips.
- **Needles:** long, thin needles for hand appliqué, such as sharps, straw, or milliner's needles. For machine appliqué, use thin needles such as size 60/8.
- **Threads:** for hand appliqué, use fine cotton thread that matches the appliqué pieces. Try medium-beige or grey for multi-coloured prints. For decorative machine appliqué, any machine embroidery thread; for blind appliqué, very fine nylon thread.

Making appliqué templates

Appliqué patterns do not include seam allowances – they are added when patches are cut. Use a photocopier to reproduce patterns, enlarging or reducing them if necessary. Glue the paper copies onto lightweight cardboard or sandpaper, then cut out on the line. If you prefer, you can trace shapes directly onto clear or opaque template plastic. Make a template for each shape in the project.

Preparing the background

Cut a background square 2.5–5 cm (1–2") longer and wider than its finished size. For simple appliqué layouts, fold and finger-press the background piece vertically, horizontally, and along its diagonals. The resulting creases mark the block's centre and equally spaced areas surrounding it, and can be used to help position appliqué pieces. For more complicated blocks, place a copy of the full pattern on a light box (see page 32).

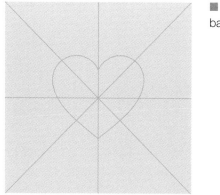

■ Preparing the background

Centre the background fabric on top of the pattern and use a pencil to trace the basic components of the layout directly onto the fabric, just inside the lines. There's usually no need to trace every line of every piece – just enough to help you position shapes accurately.

Working with curves

- Inside (concave) curves fold under more easily when clipped. Use sharp-tipped scissors to make tiny clips perpendicular to the seam allowance. Do not clip all the way to the fold line.
- Clips are not necessary for outside (convex) curves.

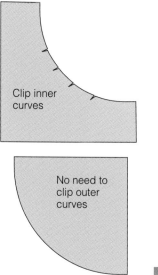

Clip inner curves

No need to clip outer curves

■ Working with curves

Needleturn appliqué

For this method, the raw edges are turned under as you sew.

1 Make a template for each different shape in the project. Position a template right-side up on the right side of fabric and trace around it with a pencil or other marker.

2 Cut out the piece, adding a 4 mm ($\frac{3}{16}$") seam allowance around all sides. Repeat steps 1 and 2 for all pieces. Trim points and clip curves if necessary.

3 Pin pieces to the background fabric, adding them from the rear forward. If thread becomes tangled in the pin ends, try pinning from the back, or use very short straight pins, called sequin pins. Another option is to baste pieces to the background.

4 Select a thread that matches the appliqué patch. Thread the needle with approximately 50 cm (20") of thread. Knot the thread and bring the needle up through the marked fold line of the piece.

Did you know?

There is no need to turn under seam allowances on edges that will be hidden under another piece. Leave the edges unsewn, or use a running stitch to secure them to the background.

5 Use the tip of the needle to fold under the seam allowance a short distance in front of the insertion point, encasing the knot in the fold. Make sure the marked line isn't visible. Hold the fold in place with your fingers.

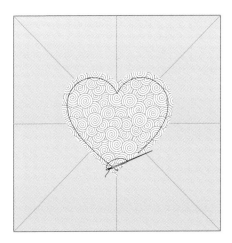

6 Insert the needle into the background fabric right next to where it came through the patch. Move the tip of the needle up through the background again, approximately 2 mm ($\frac{1}{16}$") from where it was inserted, catching a few threads of the appliqué piece as it returns. Insert the needle into the background again, and take another short stitch. Tug each stitch slightly to help hide threads. Sew in an anti-clockwise direction if you are right-handed. Reverse the direction for left-handed sewing.

7 Continue sewing around the shape, folding under only short lengths of the seam allowance at a time, until the edges are secure. If you find it difficult to fold under edges with the needle, try guiding the fabric with a toothpick.

8 After the final stitch, insert the needle through the background fabric. Take a small stitch behind the patch, and leave a loop. Insert the needle and thread through the loop and pull to tie off the thread. Clip the excess tail.

9 Appliqué the remaining pieces to the background, working forward in the design. Trim the block, squaring it up to measure 1.5 cm ($\frac{1}{2}$") larger than its finished size.

Needleturn for outside points

Sew toward the point, stopping one stitch before its end. Trim away any excess fabric that was folded under along the first side, because it will probably stick out along the opposite side of the point. Trim the fabric at the point if necessary, then fold it under carefully and continue sewing.

Needleturn for inside points

Clip inside points to the seam allowance. Stop stitching just before reaching a point, and turn under the seam allowance on the next side. Resume stitching, bringing the needle up a few threads inward from the point as you take the last stitch. Insert the needle back through the background fabric at the point, just under the edge of the appliqué. Bring it back up to take the first stitch on the next side of the shape.

Turning under edges before sewing

Try heat-resistant templates if you prefer to turn under the edges before sewing. This material resembles regular template plastic, but it will not melt under the heat of an iron. Place the template right-side down on the reverse side of the fabric and mark around it. Cut out, leaving an approximate 4 mm ($\frac{3}{16}$") seam allowance. Trim points and curves if necessary, then centre the template face down within the marked lines. Spray a little spray starch into a small cup and apply the liquid to the seam allowances with a small

brush or cotton swab. Use the tip of a dry iron to push the seam allowances over the template, drying the starch and pressing seam allowances flat. Appliqué in place on the background.

Freezer paper appliqué

For this method, patch edges are pressed to the shiny side of freezer paper before the patches are appliquéd.

1 Trace around a template placed right-side up on the non-waxy side of freezer paper. Cut out the piece on the line. Repeat to cut the total number of pieces required for each template in your design.

2 Use a hot iron to press the waxy side of the freezer paper shapes to the front side of the fabric. Cut out each shape, adding an approximate 4 mm ($\frac{3}{16}$") seam allowance around all edges.

3 Peel off the freezer paper and centre it on the wrong side of the shape, shiny-side up. Use a straight pin to secure it to the patch. Trim points and clip curves. Repeat for all pieces.

4 Use the tip of a hot, dry iron to press the seam allowance over the edges of each freezer paper shape. The fabric will adhere to the paper's softened coating. This step replaces turning under as you sew in the needleturn method.

■ Press the seam allowance over the edges of the freezer paper

Did you know?

You can avoid burning your fingers by using a toothpick or other non-heat conducting object to help fold the edges. Finger wraps are available commercially, and are a handy tool to have if you plan to appliqué often.

5 Arrange pieces on the block and appliqué. Try to avoid stitching through the freezer paper.

6 When you near the last few inches of the design, pull the freezer paper away from the shape. The seam should refold easily. Another option is to stitch all the way around each piece, and then use sharp scissors to make a small slit through the background fabric. Remove the paper through the opening.

7 Tie off threads as for needleturn appliqué. Trim and square up the block.

Sharp points with freezer paper

■ For inside points, clip to the seam line as for needleturn appliqué, then press the edges onto the freezer paper.

■ For sharp, outside points, fold the seam allowance of the point straight up across the point of the freezer paper and press. Use the tip of the iron to fold and press the seam allowance on one side of the point, then the other. Make the second fold carefully to ensure a sharp point.

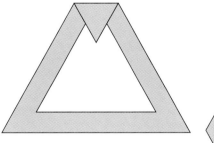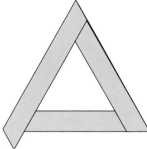

■ Achieving sharp points

Reverse appliqué

In this technique, motifs are cut from the interior of an appliqué piece and the edges are turned under at the cuts to expose another layer of fabric beneath. Window templates are a good choice for this method, because their openings allow you to mark exterior and interior lines.

1 Place a template right-side up on the right side of fabric. Mark the seamline around the patch's outer edges, and the seamlines where fabric will fold under in its interior. Cut out along the outer edge, leaving an approximate 4 mm ($\frac{3}{16}$") seam allowance. Clip inside curves and points if necessary. Cut small slits where fabric will be cut away from the shape's interior.

2 Use the template to mark (only) the outer edge of the shape on the reverse layer – the fabric that will be exposed after cut-aways are sewn. Cut out on the line. Centre the shape with seam allowances on top of the smaller, finished-size piece, both right-side up. Seam allowances should extend equally past the edges of the lower piece.

3 Appliqué the top piece to the background, encasing the reverse layer between them. Carefully trim excess fabric from the interior slits of the top layer, leaving a seam allowance extending past the seam lines. Fold under and appliqué the cut edges to expose the fabric underneath.

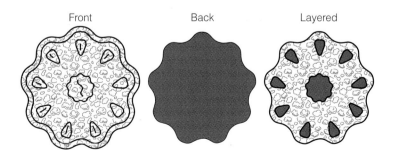

Front   Back   Layered

Sew and turn appliqué

This method eliminates the necessity for turning under raw edges. Two patches are layered and sewn right sides together, then turned inside out. For a slight three-dimensional look, cut both layers from fabric; for a sheerer look, cut one layer from non-woven interfacing – or save sheer fabric softener sheets after they've been used in a clothes dryer. This method works best with simple shapes.

1 Place a template right-side down on the reverse side of the fabric and trace around it.

2 Layer marked fabric with another fabric, right sides together. Machine sew on the line, overlapping stitches slightly at the beginning and end of the seam. Cut through both layers, leaving an approximate 4 mm ($\frac{3}{16}$") seam allowance around the patch. Clip inside corners and trim excess fabric from points.

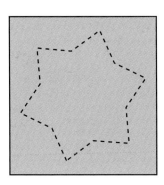

3 Make a small slit in the reverse side of the piece, then turn it right-side out. Run a point turner around the inside seam, pushing the edges out smoothly. Press and appliqué to the background.

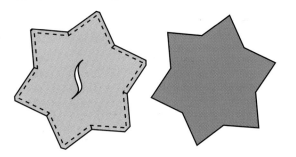

Quick fuse appliqué

Fusible web is a thin material that adheres permanently to fabric when pressed. Initially, one side is backed with paper, which protects the iron as the opposite side is fused to the fabric. Use a heavyweight fusible web if edges will not be finished with stitches. Try a lightweight product to fuse pieces if you plan to hand or machine sew around their edges. Do not wash fused projects unless the edges are finished.

1 Place a template right-side down on the paper side of the fusible web. Mark around it. Use paper scissors to cut out the shape approximately 7.5 mm ($\frac{1}{4}$") from the line.

2 Place the piece on the wrong side of the fabric, paper-side up. Follow the manufacturer's instructions to fuse it in place.

3 Cut out on the line. Cut all required pieces in the same way, then remove papers and arrange them on the background. Fuse all in place at the same time.

4 Finish the edges with decorative hand or machine stitches if you like.

Blanket stitch

1 Thread a sharp needle with one or two strands of embroidery floss, and knot one end. Bring the needle through the fabric at A, along the edge of a shape.

2 Hold the thread down with your thumb, circling it anti-clockwise. Insert the needle through the fabric at B. Bring the needle back through the fabric at C, keeping the looped thread under the point of the needle. Pull thread through and repeat.

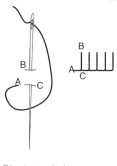

■ Blanket stitch

Did you know?

When blanket stitches are closely spaced, they are referred to as buttonhole stitches.

Machine appliqué

There are several ways to appliqué by machine. Three styles of stitch are described here. Practice these methods on scraps before you begin to sew an actual project.

Straight stitch

1 Turn under the seam allowance of the rear appliqué piece and pin it to the background. Thread a thin machine needle with matching or contrasting thread. Sew several stitches at 0 length, to anchor the thread. Gradually increase the stitch length until you are sewing 5–7 stitches per centimetre (12–15 stitches per inch). Keep sewing around the shape, decreasing stitch length as you near the end of the seam. Finish with 3–4 stitches set at 0. Do not backstitch or overlap stitches.

2 For inner and outer points, stop sewing with the needle down. Lift the presser foot and pivot to the next side of the shape. Continue sewing.

Did you know?

Bringing the bobbin thread to the surface prevents a mass of tangled threads on the reverse side. Hold on to the top thread and turn the flywheel to take one stitch, stopping the needle in the up position. Tug on the top thread to pull the bobbin thread through the fabric.

Blind stitch

A blind hem stitch is used to sew shapes to the background. With practice, this type of machine appliqué closely resembles hand appliqué. Turn under the edges of all appliqué pieces before beginning. Use a very fine nylon thread through the needle, and cotton thread in the bobbin. Choose clear nylon to sew light fabrics, smoke for darks.

1. Refer to your sewing machine owner's manual to set up a blind hem stitch. It should take several small, straight stitches, then one zigzag to the left.

2. Position the piece so that straight stitches will go through the background and the zigzag will catch the edge of the appliqué piece. Insert the needle through the background, starting on a straight side or gentle curve if possible. Bring the bobbin thread to the top and pull it out of the way.

3. Stitch around the shape, ending the seam slightly past where you began sewing.

Satin stitch

With this method, edges are appliquéd to the background with a satin stitch, a closely spaced zigzag stitch. Use a tear away stabiliser behind the background to help eliminate puckers. Machine embroidery thread is a good choice for this method.

1. Refer to your machine's manual to sew a satin stitch where stitches lie side-by-side, and are not layered on top of each other. Choose a stitch width that complements the size of your appliqué project.

2. Surround patches with the satin stitch, spacing its width so that half lies on the background and the remainder along the edge of each piece. Raw edges do not need to be turned under, because stitches will keep them intact.

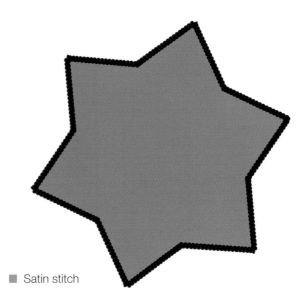

■ Satin stitch

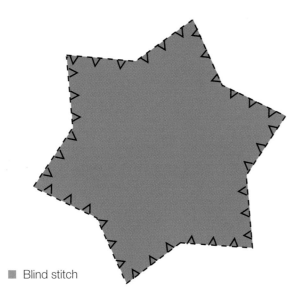

■ Blind stitch

Stained glass appliqué

This type of appliqué mimics the look of stained glass windows, where pieces of coloured glass are separated by strips of metal. In a stained glass quilt, pattern pieces are separated with narrow strips of a contrasting fabric.

Stained glass is often swirled, mottled or streaked with two or more colours. It may be crackled – as if ice had formed on its surface, or it is sprinkled with varying amounts of air bubbles. Some glasses are opaque, others are clear. You should be able to find a variety of fabrics that resemble the different kinds of glass. Incorporate fabrics that read as solids when you wish to add subtle texture to the piece. Streaked and mottled hand-dyed and Batik fabrics are a good choice for this technique.

Stained glass pattern books are a good source of designs; so are children's colouring books. Keep shapes simple, and avoid working with tiny pieces, because it would be difficult to manipulate bias strips around their edges. For a slightly different twist, try converting any traditional patchwork pattern to stained glass. If you've always wanted to make a Drunkard's Path or Eight-Pointed Star quilt, but didn't want to work with curves or set-in seams, this method may be a good alternative.

Make a cartoon

Draw a full-sized version of your pattern, called a **cartoon**, on any large sheet of paper. Freezer paper is a good choice, because pieces cut away from it later can be used as iron-on templates. Large sheets of blank newsprint are another choice. Tape sheets of paper together to draw large patterns. For freezer paper, draw on the paper side. Assign a different number to each pattern piece, including colour codes if you like.

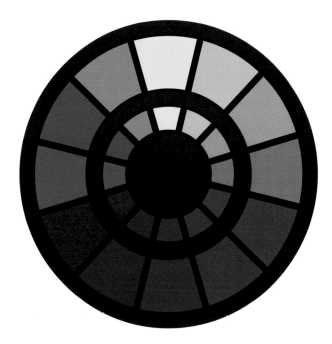

■ Stained glass colour wheel

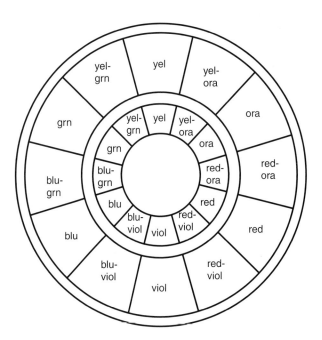

■ Cartoon drawing

appliqué

Transfer pattern to background

Stained glass quilts are built by sewing pieces to a background fabric. Prewashed muslin is a good choice. It is inexpensive, and its light colour makes marked lines easy to see. Cut out and press a piece that is 5 cm–8 cm (2"–3") longer and wider than your pattern. Spray on a little starch or sizing to stiffen the fabric, making it easier to mark. Place the fabric on top of your cartoon, both right-side up on a backlit surface (tape to a window, or use a glass table with a light under it). Trace all pattern lines onto the fabric with a pencil or permanent marker. Transfer all pattern numbers to the background.

Cut out the pieces

Cut the cartoon apart on the marked lines. Iron freezer paper templates to the right side of the fabric, or pin plain paper templates in place. Carefully cut out each piece. Do not add a seam allowance.

Put the puzzle together

Position each piece on the marked background. Pin to hold, or secure with a dab of glue. Step back and look at the overall design. Are you happy with the colour arrangement? If not, cut a few new pieces and preview your changes. Sometimes it helps to leave the room for a while: when you return, you'll see the quilt from a fresh point of view.

Baste pieces to background

Baste around the sides of each piece, placing stitches approximately 3 mm ($\frac{1}{8}$") from the edges. Stitches can be a little further inward if you plan to use wide leading. As you baste, keep in mind that half of the leading width will cover each edge.

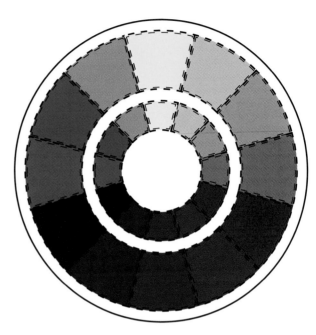

■ Baste patches in place

Did you know?

Marking lines on both sides of muslin makes it easy for you to flip the piece over, then machine sew pieces to the background. Sew just inside the marked lines.

Make the bias leading

Use the bias tube technique on page 79 to make leading strips. Quilters have traditionally used black leading for stained glass quilts, but any contrasting colour is fine. Leading of 12.5 mm ($\frac{1}{2}$") is a good general width, but the scale of your project might dictate something different. For instance, wide leading would overpower the design of a miniature quilt, and be difficult to wrap around its components.

Did you know?

Another option for bias leading is to fold and press strips in thirds, tucking one edge under another and placing the exposed raw edge against the quilt.

Apply bias tubes to quilt

Study the design to determine the best placement for bias leading. Strip ends are overlapped at junctions, so decide which edges should be sewn to the quilt first. Often, short strips are the first to be sewn, with longer strips placed over their ends. Centre leading along adjacent pieces, with half of its width covering the edges of each.

Pin small areas of leading to the quilt, then attach using a blind stitch and matching thread. Always pin and sew inner curved edges first, then gently stretch the bias to fit the outer curve. If the outer curves are attached first, bias strips on the corresponding inner curve will be puckered.

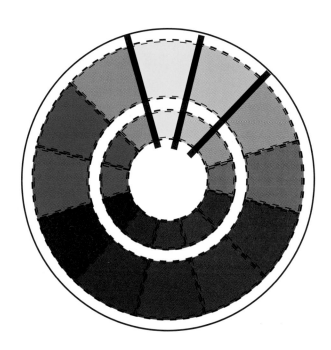

■ Add leading

Finishing

Layer the quilt with batting and backing as described on pages 98–99. Quilt as desired, and bind. Multiple blocks can be sewn together to create a large quilt.

Trim the background, leaving a seam allowance around all sides, then join in rows. When sewing identical blocks together, take care to match leading where blocks meet.

Options

■ If any one fabric is used in pieces throughout the quilt, consider using that fabric as the background. Instead of filling those areas in with individual pieces, leave them open, allowing the background to be visible.

■ Avoid basting by fusing pieces to the background with a lightweight fusible web. Follow the manufacturer's instructions when cutting and pressing pieces.

Making bias tubes

Tubes made from bias strips can be used for basket handles, and for stems that wind around floral appliqué. These flexible tubes are handy any time you want to add a narrow, graceful motif to a quilt. Use bias press bars to make the tubes. They usually come packaged in sets of several widths.

1 To determine how wide to cut strips, double the finished width of the tube, then add 1.8 cm ($\frac{3}{4}$"). Cut bias strips just as you would for binding (this is described on page 98). Use a continuous bias, or sew strips end-to-end to make one long strip.

2 Fold strips lengthwise, wrong sides together. Sew raw edges with 7.5 mm ($\frac{1}{4}$") seam allowance. Trim the seam allowance, leaving at least 3 mm ($\frac{1}{8}$").

3 Insert the press bar that matches the tube's finished width into the opening at one end of the tube. Centre the seam in the middle of the bar, face up on your ironing board. Press the seam open or to one side, using water or starch if necessary to make it lie flat. Move the bar to press all of the tube. When finished, remove the bar and press again if necessary. Cut lengths from the tube as needed for your project, and appliqué them in place.

Other techniques

There are many more types of quilts, and ways to assemble quilts, than any one book can explain. This chapter includes just a few of these 'other' techniques. Use the instructions to make a delicate throw with Yo-Yos, sew a soft, puffy bedcover in the Biscuit style, or surround a quilt with colourful Prairie Points. You can personalise any quilt by incorporating one or more of these methods into its design.

Yo-Yos

These little rosettes are made from circles of gathered fabric. They can be whipstitched side-by-side into a quilt top, with no batting or backing required. Yo-Yos can take the place of traditional floral motifs in an appliqué quilt. Sew a button at the centre to increase the three-dimensional effect. Yo-Yos work very well combined with patchwork. Arrange a bunch of Yo-Yo flowers to spill out of a basket block, placing leaves and bias vines between them if you wish.

■ This quilt combines colour with a variety of piecing and setting methods described in other chapters – now try something new

1   Make a circular template slightly larger than twice the size of the finished Yo-Yo (or mark fabric with circular kitchen objects such as jar lids and drinking glasses).

2   Mark a circle on the right side of the fabric and cut out approximately 7.5 mm ($\frac{1}{4}$") from the line. Thread a hand sewing needle with quilting thread or two strands of regular thread. Bring the needle up from the reverse side directly on the line. Turning under the seam allowance as you work, sew a continuous running stitch through both layers.

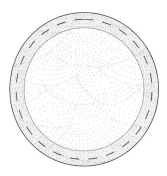

3   When you reach the starting point, pull on the thread to gather the circle, leaving a hole in the middle of the Yo-Yo. Distribute the gathers evenly, then secure them with a few backstitches.

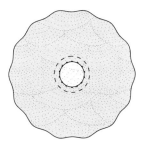

Use same-size Yo-Yos to make a quilt, table runner, or other piece where Yo-Yos are sewn side-by-side. Carefully align two Yo-Yos, gathered sides together. Take several whipstitches along one side, backstitching at the beginning and end of the seam. Continue adding Yo-Yos until you have the number required for that row. Continue adding Yo-Yos, connecting all adjacent units.

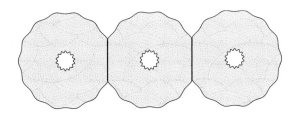

■ Making rows of Yo-Yos

For appliqué, sew Yo-Yos to the quilt with blind stitch if you wish stitches to be invisible. For extra embellishment, sew each one to the quilt with a decorative embroidery stitch.

Biscuit quilting

Two squares, one slightly smaller than the other, are sewn together and stuffed with filling, then assembled side-by-side to make a warm, puffy bedcover. The finished size of each biscuit is approximately 2.5 cm (1") smaller than the cut size of the largest square. Quilts can be scrappy, with random placement of colour and value, or have very specific designs. Develop a colour plan on graph paper before you begin, with each square representing one biscuit. Try squares of 10 cm–12.5 cm (4"–5") for a bed quilt.

1   Cut a 12.5 cm (5") square from quilt fabric, and a 11 cm (4$\frac{1}{2}$") square from the backing fabric.

2   Match and pin the four corners of the squares, wrong sides together. Pin small pleats at the midpoints on three sides, with folds flowing the same direction around the square.

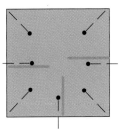

3 Use a 3 mm ($\frac{1}{8}$") seam allowance to sew the first biscuit together along its three pleated sides. Stop with the needle down at each corner, pivot, then continue sewing along the next side. Chain piece, feeding another biscuit unit through the machine without breaking threads between it and the first unit. Continue chain piecing until all the biscuits are sewn.

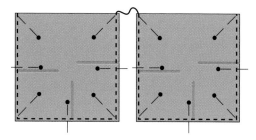

4 Stuff each unit lightly with fibrefill (if packed too full the units will be difficult to match and sew into rows). Chain sew the units together along the fourth edge, pleating again and using the same narrow seam allowance.

5 Trim threads and place two adjoining biscuits right sides together. Sew together with a 7.5 mm ($\frac{1}{4}$") seam allowance. Continue adding biscuits to complete the row. Assemble the remaining rows. Sew rows together, with seam allowances in adjacent rows finger pressed in opposite directions.

6 Make a backing to match the length and width of the quilt. Pin the backing to the quilt, right sides together. Sew a 7.5 mm ($\frac{1}{4}$") seam around the quilt, leaving an opening for turning. Turn the quilt right-side out and stitch the opening closed. Tie between biscuits at intervals across the quilt.

Prairie Points

These folded triangles are used to decorate the edges of a quilt. There are two ways to fold squares into Prairie Points, but for both the length of the finished base of the triangle is half its finished height. Use this formula to determine the beginning square size:

height of the finished point × 2, then add 1.5 cm ($\frac{1}{2}$") to the total

Method 1

Fold a square in half horizontally at its midpoint, wrong sides together. Fold each side of the square from top to bottom, creating a triangle with an open fold at its centre. Press lightly to keep folds intact. Sew this type of Prairie Point to the quilt so that when flipped upright the decorative opening will face the front.

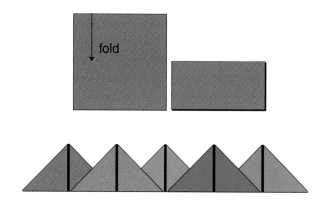

Method 2

Fold a square diagonally from corner to corner, wrong sides together. Fold again, aligning the sharp, angled edges with each other. Press lightly to keep folds intact. This method produces a Prairie Point with an open edge along one side. Tuck adjacent triangles into the opening as you distribute them along the sides of the quilt.

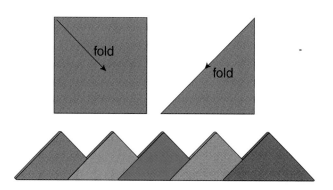

Attaching Prairie Points

Sew Prairie Points to the quilt after it has been quilted. Leave 3.75 cm (1½") free of quilting around all sides of the quilt.

1 Trim the batting and backing to match the quilt top, squaring up corners if necessary. Fold the backing and batting out of the way.

2 Position Prairie Points along one side of the quilt, right sides together. Begin at a corner and work to the opposite end of the quilt, adjusting distance to balance placement. Pin in place.

3 Sew to the quilt with a 7.5 mm (¼") seam allowance. Repeat on all sides. Trim each corner of the quilt to reduce bulk. Turn seam allowances to the back of the quilt.

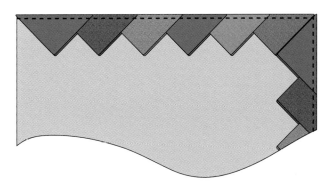

4 Fold the backing under 7.5 mm (¼"), pinning it at the base of the Prairie Points to cover the line of stitching. Blind stitch in place. Extend quilting stitches to the outer edges if necessary.

Figuring yardages

When you begin to design your own quilts, you won't have a pattern that lists required yardages. And you might decide to change a pattern, such as adding more blocks to make a larger quilt. Figuring yardage is really very simple. Just follow these basic steps. The chart on this page shows yard and metre equivalents. However, most shops will only sell fabric in 10 cm increments, so be sure to round up to the nearest 10 cm when buying fabric.

For rotary cutting

1 Most rotary-cut pieces are trimmed from long strips of fabric cut along the crosswise grain. Determine how many of each patch type you need, then divide the width of the fabric by the width or length of that patch. The answer tells you how many patches you can cut from one strip of fabric.

2 Divide the total number of patches required by the number you can cut per strip. Round up fractions to the next whole number. This is the number of strips you must cut.

3 Multiply the number of required strips by the strip width to calculate the total number of centimetres (inches) required. To calculate yardage, divide the answer by 100 cm (1 m), or 36" (1 yd).

4 Make these calculations for each piece in the quilt, keeping track of sub-totals for each fabric. Add calculations for like fabrics together, then add a little extra yardage to each to allow for shrinkage.

For template patches

Yardage for template-cut patches is calculated in the same way. Measure how much space is required to cut each patch, then proceed as above.

Yards to metres

Yards	Metres
$\frac{1}{8}$	0.12
$\frac{1}{4}$	0.23
$\frac{1}{3}$	0.30
$\frac{3}{8}$	0.36
$\frac{1}{2}$	0.46
$\frac{5}{8}$	0.56
$\frac{2}{3}$	0.60
$\frac{3}{4}$	0.68
$\frac{7}{8}$	0.80
1	0.90

10

Sets and borders

Will your quilt blocks be sewn together with their straight sides up and down, or at an angle? Will they be sewn next to other blocks? If so, what kind? Would they look best surrounded by a border? You'll be surprised by how different the same batch of quilt blocks will look when arranged in different ways. Experiment with the layout until you find the perfect setting for your quilt.

Arranging the blocks

The quilt's **set** – or **setting** – describes the way its blocks are arranged. Many blocks take on an entirely different look when their orientation is changed, so experimenting with the set is an important part of the design process.

Straight sets

In a straight-set quilt, blocks are arranged in horizontal and vertical rows. The straight edges of blocks are in the up and down position. Blocks in each row are joined, then rows are sewn together.

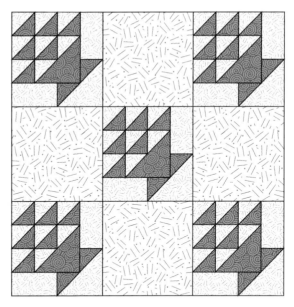

■ Straight-set with alternate blocks

■ When blocks are asymmetric, as the basket block shown here, turning them in different directions often creates a secondary design across the surface of the quilt.

■ Straight-set blocks

■ Straight-set blocks can be arranged side-by-side.
■ Plain squares, called **setting squares**, can be used between pieced blocks. Cut setting squares to match the unfinished size of the block they will be sewn next to.

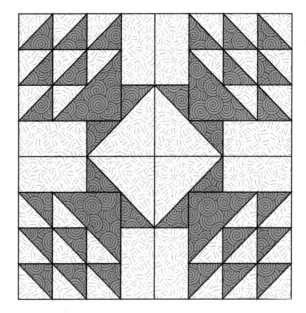

■ Asymmetrical blocks

- Simple blocks, such as the Snowball, with half-square triangles at the corners, make good alternating blocks because they link with the design in the main block to create a diagonal design that adds movement to the quilt.

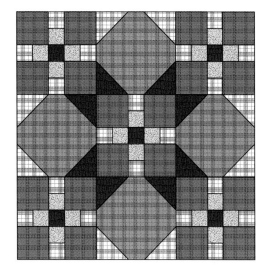

- Using connector blocks

Did you know?

Using setting squares is a quick way to increase quilt size without piecing additional blocks. Plain squares are a great place to show off your quilting talents, too.

On-point set

For an on-point set, blocks are arranged with their corners pointing up and down. Components in on-point quilts are sewn together in diagonal rows, with setting triangles added at the ends of rows to fill in the jagged outer edges. Rows are joined, then corners are added to complete the quilt. As with straight-set blocks, alternate blocks or plain setting squares can be used between the main blocks. Setting and corner triangles can be pieced, or cut from a single fabric.

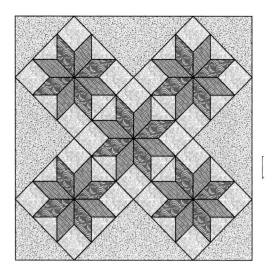

- On-point set

Medallion set

Medallion quilts have a central motif surrounded by a series of borders or other elements that relate to the design (see page 47). The central area is often on-point, with large triangles sewn to each side to create a square backdrop. This layout is a good choice for appliqué quilts, but works equally well for patchwork.

- Medallion set

Strippy set

For a strippy set, straight-set blocks are sewn into vertical columns, then separated by columns of a single fabric.

■ Strippy set

Zigzag set

For this set, blocks are placed on-point in columns. Blocks in each column are surrounded by triangles, then columns are sewn together, with or without sashing between them. Corner triangles are used at the top and bottom of each column. Setting triangles are used in between, with their long straight-grain edges facing outwards.

The Streak of Lightning set is a variation of the zigzag, in which triangles in alternate columns are offset to create a 'lightning bolt' appearance.

■ Streak of lightning set

One-patch sets

One-patch quilts contain one repeating shape. The design emerges with the quiltmaker's positioning of colour and value. Grandmother's Flower Garden is an example of a one-patch set. It looks very different when the position of dark and light fabrics are changed.

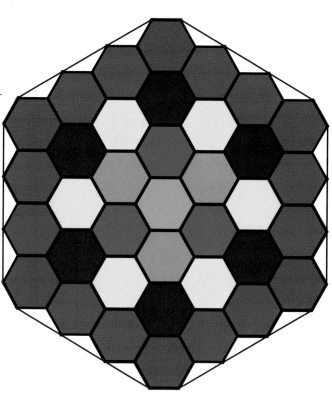

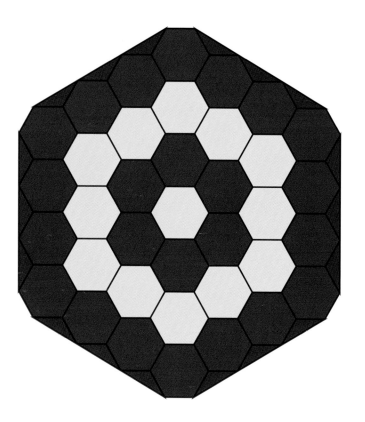

■ One-patch set showing colour variants

Setting and corner triangles

Although they are both the same shape, setting and corner triangles are cut using two different rotary-cutting methods. The correct method depends on which edges of the patch the straight grain should lie (read more about fabric grain on page 1).

Use the following formula to calculate the finished diagonal length for both types of triangles. The dimension is required to determine cut sizes for both (see below for triangle-cutting instructions):

finished diagonal = finished block size × 1.41

Cutting setting pieces for popular block sizes

Finished block size	Setting squares	Squares for setting triangles	Squares for corner triangles
10 cm × 10 cm (4" × 4")	11.5 cm × 11.5 cm (4½" × 4½")	17.75 cm × 17.75 cm (7" × 7")	9.75 cm × 9.75 cm (3¾" × 3¾")
15 cm × 15 cm (6" × 6")	16.5 cm × 16.5 cm (6½" × 6½")	24.75 cm × 24.75 cm (9¾" × 9¾")	13.25 cm × 13.25 cm (5⅛" × 5⅛")
22.5 cm × 22.5 cm (9" × 9")	24 cm × 24 cm (9½" × 9½")	35.25 cm × 35.25 cm (14" × 14")	18.5 cm × 18.5 cm (7¼" × 7¼")
25 cm × 25 cm (10" × 10")	26.5 cm × 26.5 cm (10½" × 10½")	38.75 cm × 38.75 cm (15⅜" × 15⅜")	20.25 cm × 20.25 cm (8" × 8")
30 cm × 30 cm (12" × 12")	31.5 cm × 31.5 cm (12½" × 12½")	46 cm × 46 cm (18¼" × 18¼")	23.75 cm × 23.75 cm (9⅜" × 9⅜")
35 cm × 35 cm (14" × 14")	36.5 cm × 36.5 cm (14½" × 14½")	53 cm × 53 cm (21" × 21")	27.25 cm × 27.25 cm (10¾" × 10¾")

Cutting setting triangles

Setting triangles have the straight grain running parallel to their long edge. Cut a square twice diagonally to produce four quarter-square triangles. To determine the size for the parent square, use this formula:

$$\text{size of the parent square} = \text{finished diagonal} + 3.5 \text{ cm } (1.25")$$

Round the answer up to the nearest 2.5 mm ($\frac{1}{8}$").

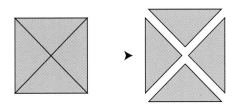

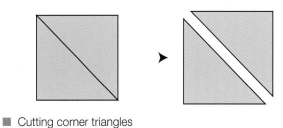

■ Cutting setting triangles

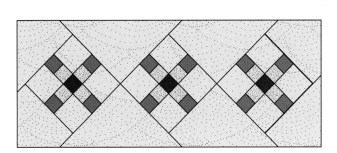

■ Floating blocks – or are they?

Cutting corner triangles

Corner triangles have the straight grain along their short edges. Cut a parent square in half once diagonally to produce two corner triangles. To determine the square size, use the following formula:

$$\text{square size} = \text{finished diagonal}/2 + 2.5 \text{ cm } (0.875")$$

Round the answer up to the nearest 2.5 mm ($\frac{1}{8}$").

■ Cutting corner triangles

Did you know?

To make blocks appear to 'float' cut larger-than-necessary setting and corner triangles from the same fabric used for the block's background.

Sashing

Plain or pieced **sashing** can be used between quilt blocks. Continuous sashing follows a simple path around blocks, with no interruptions.

■ Pieced sashing and corner squares

Continuous sashing

■ Continuous sashing

1 To make continuous sashing, determine a finished width and add 1.5 cm ($\frac{1}{2}$") for seam allowances. Cut strips that width along the lengthwise grain (crosswise grain strips are more stretchy, but can be used if necessary).

2 Cut segments from the long strips, their length equal to the unfinished size of the block. Sew segments between blocks in each row, matching as for straight-sewn borders (see page 93). Press seam allowances towards the sashing.

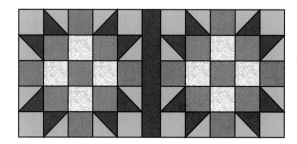

3 Add the finished width of each block in a row, plus the finished width of each sashing between blocks. Add 1.5 cm ($\frac{1}{2}$"), and use the dimension calculated to cut or sew together long sashing strips to sew between rows.

4 Sew a long strip to the bottom of each row except the last, matching as for straight-sewn borders. Sew the rows together, taking care to match vertical sashing from row to row.

5 Measure for and sew long strips of sashing to the outer edges of the quilt in the same way as for straight-sewn borders.

■ Sashing with corner squares

Sashing with corner squares

Another option is to add plain or pieced corner squares between short sections of sashing.

■ The length of each sashing unit, plain or pieced, equals the unfinished size of the block.
■ Corner squares equal the unfinished width of the sashing.
■ Sew together into rows, then connect the rows.

Borders

Borders frame the quilt, and help unify all design elements. They also perform an important structural task, acting as anchors that can help square up a slightly skewed quilt. Do not cut border strips until your quilt top is completely pieced, because its actual dimensions will probably vary a bit from the drafted size.

I don't usually select a border fabric until the top is pieced, because most fabrics look very different when cut into small segments – there have been too many occasions when a border I thought would be perfect for a quilt did not work as well as I had hoped. When a quilt top is finished, I preview several fabrics by placing uncut lengths along its sides. It's a good idea to take the quilt along if you must shop for border fabric. Most people who work in quilt shops are quilters themselves, and can often help you make a good choice.

■ Borders can be straight sewn, with edges flush against each other or mitred, with 45° angles where they meet.
■ They can be simply or intricately pieced.
■ Blocks or squares can be inserted at their corners.
■ They can be scalloped all the way around or rounded only at the corners.
■ Borders do not have to be identical on all sides.
■ In other words, let your imagination soar!

from the quilt by another fabric, so that it doesn't blend into same-fabric patches along the quilt edge?

- Do you plan to do extensive quilting in the borders? If so, a wider border will provide more space.

- Is the quilt 'busy', with lots of piecing? If it is, pieced borders may detract from the design. But a pieced border offset by plain borders might be perfect, and help continue the design to the outer edges of the quilt.

Making long borders

Borders for small or miniature quilts are easy to cut by folding fabric once or twice and using regular rotary techniques to slice away strips. Longer borders are a little different, because it's difficult to make accurate cuts through several folds. Lengthwise grain strips make the most stable borders, and can be cut in one piece if the yardage is long enough. Crosswise grain strips are a little stretchier, but can be used if yardage is short.

Either type can be pieced to make long borders. Some quilters sew strips end-to-end; others prefer to sew them together diagonally – as you do when joining binding strips – so that the seam is distributed over a longer distance. Use whichever technique works best with the border fabric you are using.

Cutting lengthwise grain strips

- Start cutting on the right-hand side of the yardage, slightly further inward than the width of the border. Cut short sections at a time, moving the fabric along the mat as you work. Cut in small steps for best accuracy, leaving a portion of the ruler matched to a short length of the previous cut. Turn the border around to trim the opposite side.
- Measure and mark the fabric carefully, then cut with scissors.
- Tear borders along the lengthwise grain. Not everyone likes to tear fabric, but it usually produces a straight edge.

Border width

You will probably see a different recommendation for border widths in each quilting book that you read, but there isn't a standard formula to determine border width. You are the only one who can select the best border width for your quilt. Here are a few points to consider when designing borders.

- How many total borders will you use? Do you want to frame a piece with a very narrow accent border, then add one or more wider borders around it?
- Would you like to repeat a fabric used in the quilt? If so, would a wide or narrow strip enhance the layout best? Should the fabric be separated

Making straight-sewn borders

1 To determine side border length, measure the quilt top from top to bottom through its vertical midpoint. *Never* measure the outer edges of the quilt, because they are often stretched out of shape a little by the time the quilt top is assembled.

2 Cut or piece together strips to make two side borders that match the length determined in step 1. Fold a border in half crosswise and crease to mark its midpoint. Pin the midpoint to the horizontal midpoint of the quilt, matching edges with right sides together. Match and pin at the ends, and then continue pinning along the entire length of both pieces. Pin at close intervals to ease in fullness if necessary.

3 Sew the border to the quilt with a 7.5 mm ($\frac{1}{4}$") seam allowance. If you had to ease in fullness (step 2), sew with the longer piece next to the feed dogs. Add the border to the opposite side of the quilt in the same way. Press seam allowances toward the borders.

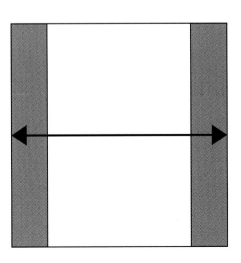

4 To determine top and bottom border length, measure the quilt top from side-to-side through its horizontal midpoint, including the side borders. Cut or piece two borders that length.

5 Fold a border in half crosswise and crease. Placing right sides together, pin the midpoint to the vertical midpoint at the top edge of the quilt. Match and pin the ends next, and continue pinning just as you did for the side borders. Sew the border to the quilt with a 7.5 mm ($\frac{1}{4}$") seam allowance. Add the bottom border. Repeat all steps if you wish to add another layer of borders to the quilt.

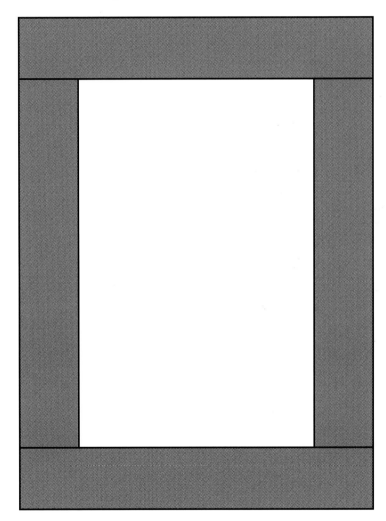

Did you know?

When you fold-match, fold adjacent units in opposite directions, one right sides together, the other wrong sides together. When matched for sewing, the folds will nest into each other to help you achieve a perfect match.

Making mitred borders

Mitred borders can be used anytime, but they are a good choice for directional fabrics such as stripes, which look best if corners are matched so that the design flows in a continuous stream around the quilt.

1   Measure the quilt through its vertical and horizontal midpoints. To each of those figures, add twice the finished width of the border, plus 10 cm (4"). Cut two borders each length.

2   Fold a border crosswise to find its midpoints. On the edge that will be aligned for sewing, mark the midpoint with a pin, and then measure outward along the border to pin-mark the ending length of the quilt on each side (use the measurements determined in step 1). *Do not* match the border to the side of the quilt to determine length. Repeat with the remaining borders.

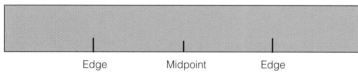

Edge   Midpoint   Edge

3   Beginning exactly at a marked end point, align a ruler to draw a 45° diagonal line to represent the finished seam line where borders will be joined at the corners. Mark a second line parallel to and 7.5 mm (¼") past the first. This is the cutting line – but do not cut until borders are sewn to the quilt. Repeat on the opposite end of the strip and on remaining borders.

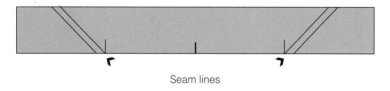

Seam lines

4   Align a border to the quilt as for straight-sewn borders, pinning midpoints and end marks first and then pinning along an entire side.

5   Sew the border to the quilt between pin marks. Use a 7.5 mm (¼") seam allowance, backstitching at stop and start points. Do not sew into the seam allowance at either end.

6   Repeat steps 4 and 5 to sew the remaining borders to the quilt.

7   Fold quilt corners diagonally, right sides together. Match and pin the marked sewing lines at one corner. The end points of adjacent seams should match. Begin sewing at the spot where the previous seams ended. Backstitch, then continue sewing to the ends of strips. Trim the marked cutting line and press seam open. Repeat on remaining corners.

Did you know?

If you are using more than one mitred border, you can sew all strips for each side together lengthwise, then add the unit to the quilt as one piece. For easier matching where strips meet at mitres, press seam allowances in the side borders in the opposite direction to the seam allowances in the top and bottom borders.

Borders with corner blocks or squares

1   Choose a finished border width and add 1.5 cm (½") to allow for seams. Measure the quilt top vertically and horizontally as for straight-sewn borders. Cut two border strips for each length. If the ends of more than one border will touch the corner block, cut the remaining borders the same lengths and sew the strips side-by-side to add as one unit.

2   Sew the side borders to the quilt, aligning them as described for straight-sewn borders. Press the seam allowances toward the borders.

3   Cut or piece corner squares equal to the *finished* width of the border, plus a total of 1.5 cm (½") for seam allowances. Sew a corner square to each end of the top and bottom borders. Press the seam allowances toward the borders.

4 Sew the top and bottom borders to the quilt, matching midpoints, ends and seam intersections first and then matching along the entire side of each. Press seam allowances toward the borders.

that seem complex but are really very simple. For easy calculations, use triangle squares that finish at the same size as an individual unit in your blocks.

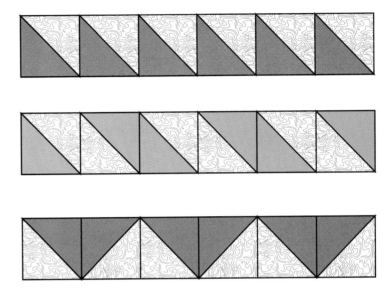

■ Pieced borders

String-pieced borders

Make foundations slightly longer than each border dimension, then string piece on them. Press, trim excess fabric from edges, and trim to the correct length. Add interest by using strings in a variety of widths and angles.

Appliqué borders

Appliqué any shapes you desire to plain or pieced borders after they are sewn to the quilt. Leave at least 2.5 cm (1") free around the outer edges of the borders. For floral designs, try winding narrow stems made with bias bars throughout the design.

Scalloped edges look great with appliqué borders. Use a compass or any circular shape to draw a curved template. Sew borders to the quilt, then align the curve to the sides, mark and cut. Appliqué shapes to the borders.

Pieced borders

Borders can be pieced as simply or intricately as you desire. Ensure the layout is planned so that units fit evenly onto both sides. Triangle-square units can be combined in many ways to make attractive borders

11

Finishing the quilt

After the quilt top is assembled, it's time to mark it for quilting and to layer it with batting and backing – creating what is often called the **quilt sandwich**. The final step is binding – when everything you have worked to achieve comes together to create a special quilt.

Did you know?

In the USA, the filling used for quilts is called **batting**. *In the UK, many quilters use the term* **wadding**.

Getting ready to quilt

Quilting designs are marked before the quilt top is sandwiched with batting and backing. Ensure that the quilt is pressed before marking to avoid heat-setting the lines. Test your marker on scrap fabric first, then launder to make sure the marks will wash out. There are several alternatives for marking:

- Mark lightly with a sharp, hard lead pencil (H or 2H; #3 or #4). Several companies produce mechanical pencils for quilters, which have a very fine, slightly different, lead that is easier to remove after the quilt is complete.
- Artist's pencils are another choice. They are available in many colours, allowing you to choose shades that will contrast with fabrics in the quilt. Berol Verithin pencils are a good choice if you can get hold of them.

- Mark with chalk. Try chalk pencils, tailor's chalk, or special tools that apply a thin line of powder to the cloth. Chalk lines rub off easily, so you will probably need to mark small sections as you work, after the quilt is sandwiched.
- The lines from soapstone pencils rub off easily without leaving a residue. These light-coloured markers are best for marking dark fabrics.

Choose a quilting design

A number of designs are possible, and a few are described here.

Use the motifs on **pre-cut quilting stencils**, or draw your own on template plastic. Cut out the design with a double-bladed craft knife or stencil burner.

Draw quilting designs **on freezer paper**. Cut out a shape and press it lightly to the sandwiched quilt top. Quilt around the paper, and then pull it away and press to another area.

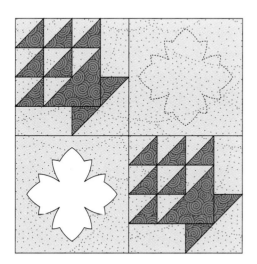

■ Using a freezer paper pattern

Outline quilt 7.5 mm ($\frac{1}{4}$") from seams. Narrow, 6 mm ($\frac{1}{4}$"), masking tape makes a good guide for straight areas, and is pliable enough to wrap around gentle curves. When one area is finished, move the tape to

the next section to be quilted. Straight lines can also be marked with pencils, using a rotary ruler as a guide.

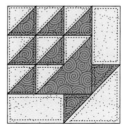

■ Outline quilting

In-the-ditch quilting is done alongside a seam or appliqué edge. No marking is necessary.

Echo quilting is often used for appliqué quilts. Shapes are quilted in-the-ditch, then outlined 6 mm ($\frac{1}{4}$") away. Additional, equally spaced lines radiate outward from the shape.

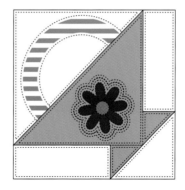

■ Echo quilting

Tear-away designs are handy for machine quilting. Designs are printed on paper, which is pinned to the sandwiched quilt. After quilting, the paper is removed.

Instead of quilting specific shapes, decorate with **all-over quilting lines**. This type of quilting covers the entire quilt without regard to its components. Typical designs include:

- Continuous, diagonal lines.
- Crosshatching, which is made up of straight lines running at 45° to each other.
- Diamonds, similar to crosshatching, but with a deeper angle.
- Clamshells.

When this type of quilting stops at certain quilt components, allowing them to bulge out from the surface, it is called **background quilting**.

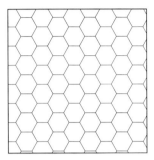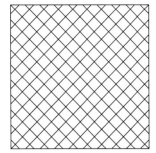

■ Background quilting

Did you know?

Try an all-over design from the back, quilting along the lines of a printed backing fabric.

Stipple quilting is composed of closely spaced, curved lines that meander across the surface, never touching each other. **Meander quilting** is similar, but the lines are further apart. Premarking is not required for either of these freehand designs.

■ Stipple/meander quilting

Backing

The reverse side of a quilt can be made from a single fabric, or it can be pieced in a more decorative way. You can even back the quilt with another quilt, making it reversible – but do keep in mind that there will be double the amount of seam allowances to quilt through.

Backings are usually 10–20 cm (4–8") wider and longer than the quilt. Quilts measuring less than 100 cm (40") wide can be backed with a single panel of 110 cm (44") fabric. Fabric manufacturers now offer a good selection of wide backing fabrics for larger quilts, but it's easy to piece a simple backing if you prefer.

Making the backing

1 Measure the quilt horizontally and vertically. Add 10–20 cm (4–8") to each measurement. Decide how many panels you will use, and if the seams will be horizontal or vertical.
2 Remove the selvages from fabric. Determine the strip widths required to piece the configuration you have chosen. Cut panels 1.5 cm ($\frac{1}{2}$") wider than the required size. Sew them together.
3 Press seam allowances open if you intend to hand quilt.

Did you know?

A multi-coloured print backing camouflages gaps left by missed stitches on the back side of the quilt.

Batting

Quilt battings are divided into two general categories: natural and synthetic. Wool, cotton, and silk are all natural fibres; polyester is synthetic. Visit your local quilt shop and read the labels to learn more about batting characteristics and care. Some shops and mail-order companies offer batting-swatch samples to help you make comparisons. Make sure that you read the labels to find out how closely each batting must be quilted.

■ Wool drapes nicely and is easy to quilt by hand or machine. Wool retains its loft, because its barbed structure allows the fibres to spring back to their original shape after compression.

- 100% cotton batting is usually more difficult to hand quilt, but is easy to quilt by machine. For hand quilting, look for **needlepunched** versions. This process breaks up and interlocks the fibres, making hand quilting easier.
- Batts blended from 80% cotton and 20% polyester provide good needling for hand quilters and do not need to be as closely quilted as pure cotton batts.
- Polyester batts are easy to hand quilt. One disadvantage is that they tend to **beard**, meaning that fibres migrate through the cloth and onto the top and backing of your quilt. Quilting at close intervals helps keep bearding in check.

Select a batting that suits the quilt:

- Miniature quilts generally look best with thin battings. Wallhangings do too, as they must lie flat against a wall. If you can't find anything thin enough to suit you, peel a batting in half to make it thinner.
- Cotton batts are good for bed quilts, for the same reason cotton fabrics are – they breathe, providing warmth in winter but staying cool in warmer months.
- Thick polyester batts are a good choice for decorative comforters that will be tied.
- Choose a thin, 100% cotton batting for a vintage look.

Making the quilt sandwich

1 Place the backing right-side down on a smooth, flat surface. Some quilters like to pull the backing taut, and hold it in place with strips of masking tape; others simply smooth it out. Stretching is most important for machine quilting, because it makes the reverse side of the quilt run through the machine with less chance of puckers.

2 Pre-shrink the batting if necessary, following the manufacturer's instructions. Centre the batting on top of the backing, smoothing the folds. If creases persist, allow the batting to rest for a while, or tumble it in a cool dryer for a few minutes.

3 Trim stray threads that remain on the quilt top. Centre the quilt right-side up on top of the batting, and smooth it in place.

4 Now it's time to **baste**, the process which holds the three layers of the quilt together. For hand quilting, baste the layers with thread. Use a darning needle and white or neutral thread: colours in threads sometimes stain fabrics. Take long stitches through all layers, enough to keep the layers from shifting as the quilt is handled. For machine quilting, baste with rustproof safety pins. Place pins 7.5–12.5 cm (3–5") apart and leave them open until all are in place. Minimise hole size by using as small a pin as you can comfortably place through the layers. Tacking guns are another basting option – these devices are like the tools department stores use to apply plastic tags to clothing.

5 Machine or hand quilt.

Did you know?

The serrated edges of a grapefruit spoon can be used to close safety pins, helping to eliminate sore fingers.

Hand quilting

Needles

Hand quilting is accomplished using short, sturdy needles called **betweens**. In general, the smaller the needle, the smaller your stitches will be. Start with a size 9 or 10, then switch to a smaller size 12 when you feel comfortable with the stitch.

Thread

Hand quilting thread is stronger than all-purpose sewing thread. If you must quilt with all-purpose thread, coat it with beeswax, which is available in most quilting shops.

- Thread has a grain, and flows more smoothly through the cloth in one direction than it does in the other. To take advantage of this, knot the end of thread that came off the spool last.

Quilting frames

Frames and hoops hold the layers of the quilt together, keeping them from shifting as you quilt. The quilt can be adjusted loosely or can be held taut, whichever you prefer.

- Quilts are stretched to their full size in floor frames. No basting is required. The edges of the quilt are held in place by the frame. Floor frames aren't as popular as they were in the past, because most people don't have the extra space to devote to large frames.
- Roller frames allow you to work on large sections of the quilt at a time, but take up much less space than floor frames. Basting is not required with some types.
- Hoops are usually round or oval, and most are made from wood. Some have a base that sits on your lap, or on a table in front of you. Move the hoop around to quilt different areas.

Thimbles and finger guards

Thimbles are used on top of the quilt to guide the needle downwards. You use a finger on your other hand to detect the needle as it emerges on the back of the quilt. That finger will callous over time from repeated pricking, unless you shield it with something. A few layers of masking tape work well, but a growing number of finger guards are available commercially. Use a guard thin enough to let you feel the needle, but thick enough to keep its point from piercing your skin.

The quilting stitch

1 Thread a needle with approximately 45 cm (18") of thread. Knot the end by wrapping the thread's tail around the needle a few times. Pull the needle through the wraps, holding them with your fingers. Keep pulling until the wrapped threads are at the end of the strand.

2 Insert the needle through the quilt top approximately 2.5 cm (1") from where you plan to start quilting. *Do not* go through to the backing. Bring the needle back up directly on a quilting line and tug the thread to pop the knot into the batting.

3 Position the needle so that it is perpendicular to the quilt's surface. Let it move downward, but do not push it with the thimble. When you feel the tip of the needle on the underneath side, push it upward towards the top of the quilt. Move it downward again to take another stitch. Use a rocking motion to load several stitches on the needle, then push its head to the surface with your thimble. Pull the needle through the quilt top.

4 To end a line of stitching, bring the needle up through the fabric just past the final stitch. Make a loop as the last length of thread comes through the top, and form a knot about 7.5 mm ($\frac{1}{4}$") away from the quilt top. Insert the needle into the quilt top, directly where the thread is coming out. Bring the needle back through the quilt top about 2.5 cm (1") away, tugging to pop the thread into the batting. Cut the thread flush with the quilt top. Begin quilting where the last stitch ended, or in a new area.

Did you know?

There is a product called Tiger Tape, which has evenly spaced lines printed on masking tape. Used as a quilting guide, the lines help you make evenly spaced stitches.

Tying a quilt

Tying is a fast and easy way to finish a quilt, and is an attractive way to finish a comforter filled with thick batting. The batting will be pulled tight at the ties, and billow out around them. Use a batting that will not separate when the quilt is washed. Bonded or needlepunched polyester batts are good choices. Ties should be no more than 10 cm (4") apart.

1 Sandwich the quilt and baste it with straight pins.
2 Thread a darning needle with a long length of yarn, perle cotton, or strands of embroidery floss.
3 From the top of the quilt, take a small stitch through all layers. Bring the needle up through the layers and pull thread through, leaving a tail of 8–10 cm (3–4").
4 Move to the next tie position and take another stitch through the layers. Bring the needle up, leaving long, loose layers of yarn between the stitches. The loose yarn will eventually be cut in half, leaving tails that are tied together at each stitch. Continue stitching across the surface of the quilt.
5 Cut yarn between stitches in half. Tie tails together at each stitch with two square knots. Trim loose tails to equal lengths.

For less visible ties, work from the reverse side of the quilt, and make knots there.

Machine quilting

Machine quilting is becoming more and more popular with quilters. It can resemble traditional hand quilting, or stand out boldly on the surface of the quilt. As with hand quilting, stitches can be in straight lines, graceful curves, or meander casually across the layout.

Threads and needles

For machine quilting that resembles hand quilting, use a very fine nylon thread through the needle, such as the product available from YLI. Nylon stitches are visible as indentations, but the thread itself is more difficult to see. Clear nylon is best for light fabrics, smoke for darker fabrics.

For more visible stitches, sew with lightweight cotton threads, or choose something from the growing number of decorative threads available. Metallic threads, and thin, flat slivers of transparent lamé both add shimmer to a quilt. Variegated threads are another choice, and give resulting quilting lines a subtle to dramatic colour change along their length.

Use lightweight cotton thread in the bobbin. Another choice is lingerie thread, which is lightweight but strong. It works especially well when you are sewing with a heavier, decorative thread through the needle.

Use a new needle made especially for machine quilting. These needles have a large eye, which is designed to stay cooler than a regular needle would when passed through multiple layers at a high speed. If your thread breaks or splits apart, try a machine embroidery needle, with an even larger eye. If threads continue to split, apply a stream of thread lubricant from top to bottom along the spool of thread.

Make a practice piece

Assemble a 30 cm × 30 cm (12" × 12") practice piece that contains the same backing and batting you're using in your quilt. Use a single piece of fabric to replace the quilt top. Pin baste if you like, but be sure to remove the pins as you come to them. Try both of the techniques described below before you begin quilting the quilt. Make additional practice pieces and experiment with stitches until you feel comfortable with the techniques. Use contrasting threads in the needle and bobbin.

Straight-line quilting

Straight-line machine quilting is best accomplished with a **walking foot**, also called an even-feed foot. This specialised presser foot grips the top of the quilt to advance it through the machine at the same rate as the backing, which is moved along by the feed dogs. It keeps layers from shifting apart as they are sewn, so reduces distortion and pleats on the front and back of the quilt. Gentle curves are possible with the walking foot, but reserve intricate patterns for free-motion techniques.

When you use a walking foot, the feed dogs are up, just as they are for normal sewing. Stitch length is controlled by the machine's settings. This technique is perfect for grid, in-the-ditch, and outline quilting. You can stop with the needle down, and pivot the piece as you would for other sewing tasks.

1 Mark the top for quilting and pin baste the layers. Position the walking foot and needle at the beginning of the first quilting line. Take one stitch and lift the presser foot. Tug on the top thread slightly, to bring a loop of the bobbin thread to the surface. Use a seam ripper or long straight pin to catch the loop and pull it all the way out of the quilt.

2 Take 6–10 very short stitches, then gradually lengthen them to the desired length as you sew the remaining portion of the line. As you near the end of the line, reduce the stitch length again, taking 6–10 very short stitches at its end. The short stitches lock the end points in place, so tying off isn't necessary. Carefully clip thread ends very close to the surface of the quilt.

Free-motion machine quilting

Free-motion quilting is done with a darning foot, or a similar specialized foot with a larger opening. The feed dogs are placed in the down position, so the quilter controls stitch length by needle speed and the rate at which the quilt is moved under the needle. Stitches can be random or follow a marked line. Free-motion quilting takes practice, but once you've mastered it there's no limit to the designs you can achieve.

1 Move the feed dogs to the down position. Take one stitch and pull the bobbin thread to the surface.

2 Place your hands on each side of the piece and press the foot control to the floor. This technique works best when you run the machine at a fast, consistent speed. When you're beginning to learn free-motion quilting, set the machine to sew half-speed if possible: it slows the needle down a bit, but allows you to floor the machine to keep the speed consistent. Take several very small stitches to seat the seam.

3 Move the piece under the needle. Stitch length is controlled solely by the speed and direction of your movements. This technique takes a lot of practice, so don't worry if your stitches are irregular at first. Experiment with freehand motions before you attempt to follow a marked line. End a line of stitching by taking several short stitches to lock off the seam.

Tension settings

After you've sewn a few lines, examine the front and back of your piece. The bobbin thread should be visible on the reverse side of the block, the top thread on the top. It's fine if very small dots of either thread show on the 'wrong' side, but if large amounts of either thread have been pulled to the wrong side you must adjust the tension.

■ If too much top thread has been pulled to the back, make the top tension stronger.

■ If too much bobbin thread has been pulled to the front, make the top tension weaker. Monitor tension settings closely as you quilt.

Squaring up the quilt

Sometimes it is necessary to square up the corners of the quilt before binding is applied. Use a large square ruler at the top of each corner, and very carefully cut away small areas that may have been distorted during quilting. Be sure to leave a 7.5 mm ($\frac{1}{4}$") seam allowance on all sides of pieced blocks that surround the perimeter of the quilt.

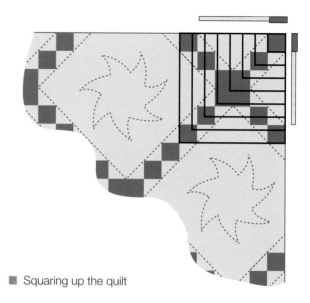

■ Squaring up the quilt

Binding

Binding covers the raw edges of the quilt sandwich. It can blend or contrast with the quilt or borders, can be narrow or wide, depending on the look you want to achieve. You can repeat a fabric used within the quilt or select an entirely new one.

Strip selection

- Lengthwise grain strips should not be used for binding, because their straight threads would run parallel to the edge of the quilt. A single thread, weakened from heavy use, could split the binding apart on an entire side of the quilt.
- Most crosswise grain strips do not run exactly with the grain, so there's less risk of long splits. Strips have enough stretch to flow around large curves, but are not the best choice for binding tight curves or deep angles.
- The grain in bias binding runs from front to back at an angle, so if a single thread weakens, the binding will split in a much smaller area. It is ideal for quilts with deeply curved or angled edges.

Doublefold binding (French binding)

Doublefold binding is made from a strip of fabric folded lengthwise to make two layers. It is durable, and offers good protection for quilt edges. If threads in the upper layer split, the lower layer usually remains intact long enough for repairs to be made. Use the following formula to calculate strip width.

$$\text{strip width} = 2 \times (3 \times \text{finished binding width} + \text{seam allowance})$$

Add a little extra for quilts with thick batting.

Singlefold binding

Singlefold binding contains one layer of fabric. Use it for miniatures or small wallhangings, but not for bed quilts where durability is important. Use the following formula to calculate strip width, adding a little extra width if thick batting is used.

$$\text{strip width} = 3 \times \text{finished binding width} + 2 \times \text{seam allowance}$$

Wide bindings

If your quilt does not have borders, the final seam around its perimeter will probably need to be sewn 7.5 mm ($\frac{1}{4}$") from all sides. Sewing a wider seam will travel too far inward on blocks, and result in inaccurate patches around the outside edges of the quilt. To use a wide binding, square up the quilt top, folding the batting and backing out of the way before trimming each side. Subtract 7.5 mm ($\frac{1}{4}$") from the finished width of the binding, and trim the batting and backing to extend past all edges of the quilt by that width. Sew the binding to the edges of the quilt top in the normal way, using a 7.5 mm ($\frac{1}{4}$") seam allowance. The increased width shows when you take the binding to the back of the quilt, because the binding must fold over the excess batting and backing extending along each side.

■ Wide bindings

Narrow bindings

If you plan to sew a 7.5 mm ($\frac{1}{4}$") binding seam, then trim it back to a narrower width, make mitred folds at each corner (see mitring instructions, page 105) based on the final width of the binding. For instance, for a binding you will trim back to 3 mm ($\frac{1}{8}$") begin each fold 3 mm ($\frac{1}{8}$") inward from the quilt's edges rather than folding the binding so that it is flush with the quilt. Larger folds create too much bulk at mitres.

Sewing binding strips end-to-end

Strips can be joined end-to-end to make long lengths of binding. Place strips right sides together, perpendicular to each other. Mark the top strip on the diagonal and then sew a seam on the line. Cut off the excess fabric, leaving a 7.5 mm ($\frac{1}{4}$") seam allowance. Press the seam open and trim nubs left by the excess seam allowance. Join additional strips until binding is the correct length.

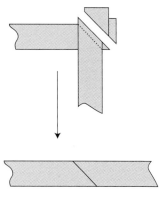

■ Sewing binding strips end-to-end

Continuous bias binding

Bias binding can be cut in one long string when you start with a square of fabric. To determine how much bias a square will produce, find the area of the square by multiplying its length by its width, then use this formula:

length produced = area of square divided by width of binding strip

To estimate square size based on the length of binding required, multiply the length of strip required by the width of the strip to find the area of the strip. The square root of that area gives you the square size needed.

1   Cut a large square from binding fabric. Use pins to mark two opposite edges. Cut the square diagonally from one corner to the other.

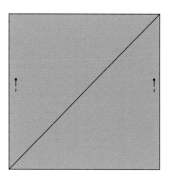

2   Use a 7.5 mm ($\frac{1}{4}$") seam allowance to sew the two pin-marked edges right sides together.

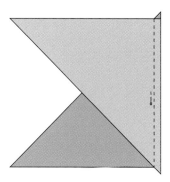

3   Press the seam open. Mark lines on the reverse side of the fabric, parallel to the long edges. Space lines equal to the distance of the cut width of binding.

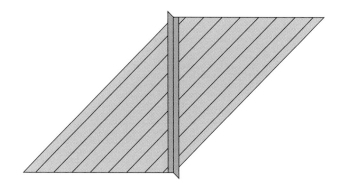

4 Make a tube by bringing the right sides of the fabric together, offsetting ends so that lines match exactly. Sew the ends together and press the seam open.

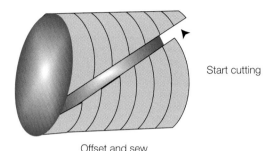

Start cutting

Offset and sew

5 Start cutting at either side of the tube, on a marked line. Continue cutting around the tube to make one long continuous strip of bias binding.

This method works better with large pieces of fabric, since using small squares will result in many seam allowances along the length of the strip.

Doublefold mitred binding

1 Measure the quilt vertically and horizontally. Add these measurements together and multiply by two. Add 38 cm (15") and make your binding that length. Strip width is determined by the type of binding you use.

2 Align the raw edge of the binding with an edge on the front side of the quilt. Do not start in a corner. Pin the binding along the side, leaving a 7.5 cm (3") tail loose at the beginning. Align the binding with the rest of the quilt, without pinning, to make sure its seam allowances will not end up in a corner, where they will create too much bulk. If they do, shift the start point to another area.

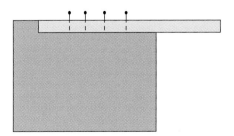

3 Sew the binding to the quilt using the seam width chosen earlier. Stop sewing before you reach the corner, ending your seam the same distance from the edge as the width of the seam allowance. Backstitch and remove the quilt from the machine.

4 Fold the long end of the binding straight up over the seam you sewed in step 3, positioning it so that it is parallel to the next side of the quilt. There will be a 45° angle on the strip's lower right edge. Fold the binding down again, the fold flush with the top of the quilt and raw edges aligned with the sides. The angle should still be intact underneath the folded edge.

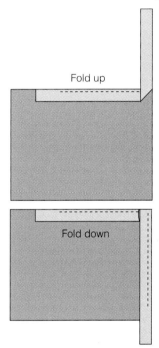

Fold up

Fold down

5 Pin the binding to the next side and continue sewing, beginning where the previous seam ended. Backstitch at the start of the seam.

6 End the next seam the same distance from the corner as the first. Backstitch. Mitre the corner as before and continue sewing along the next side. Treat each corner in the same way.

7 On the last side, stop sewing 10 cm–15 cm (4"–6") from the starting point. Backstitch. Trim the end of the tail, leaving it long enough to overlap the unsewn tail at the start by about 10 cm (4").

finishing the quilt

8 Beginning at the raw edge, make a 45° cut in the starting tail. Lay the ending tail under the angled starting tail. Draw a line next to and matching the diagonal cut. Add a 1.5 cm (½") seam allowance to the diagonal edge of the ending tail and trim.

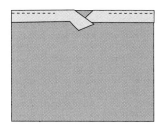

9 Place the angled tails right sides together, offsetting ends by 7.5 mm (¼"). Sew together with a 7.5 mm (¼") seam allowance. Pin and sew the last section of binding to the quilt.

10 Beginning on one side, take the folded edge of the binding to the back of the quilt. It should fit snugly over the quilt's edge. Hold in place with pins, or use special binding clips, which resemble hair barrettes. Mitres will form automatically at front corners, and can be easily folded at corners on the reverse side. Use a blind stitch and matching thread to sew the binding to the back of the quilt. Take a few stitches in each mitre to hold it in place.

Singlefold binding is mitred in the same way. Turn under the raw edge as the binding is folded to the back of the quilt. Hand stitch along the fold.

Tucked ends for doublefold binding

Try this method to finish binding ends:

1 Unfold the binding and cut a 45° angle at the beginning end. Press an approximate 7.5 mm (¼") seam in the angled edge, wrong sides together. Keep the strip unfolded, and sew about 7.5 cm (3") only of its bottom edge to the quilt.

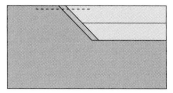

2 Stop sewing and lift the presser foot. Fold the binding in half again, aligning the top raw edge with the lower raw edge. Lower the presser foot and continue sewing through both layers.

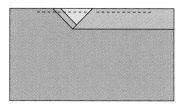

3 Sew binding to the quilt, mitring the corners. When you near the starting point stop sewing, leaving the needle in the down position. Trim the ending tail if necessary and tuck it into the opening at the starting point. Continue stitching through all thicknesses until all edges of the binding are sewn to the quilt. Now use blind stitch and matching thread to sew the strips together along the angled edge.

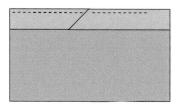

Straight-sewn binding

Use four singlefold strips of fabric, sewing each to the quilt independently. Sew the binding to the two opposite sides first, and then fold edges under and blind stitch to the back. Trim flush with the sides of the quilt. Sew the two remaining strips to the quilt. Blind stitch to the back, turning under the raw edges at the ends and overlapping the first binding on each side.

Doublefold binding is not recommended for this method because it creates too much bulk at overlapped ends.

Did you know?

Some quilters like to sew binding to the quilt before the excess batting and backing are trimmed away because that makes certain the binding will be filled to its edge with all three materials. Try both methods to see which you like best.

Binding curves and angles

- Some quilters prefer to use a single thickness of bias binding around curves.
- Ease the binding around outer curves. If it is stretched, the curves will cup when the quilt is complete.
- Raise the presser foot at the inside junctions of curves, taking a few stitches and manipulating layers to keep puckers from forming.

Self binding

To make a self binding, sometimes called a **rolled binding**, select a fabric backing that complements the quilt. Move the backing out of the way and trim the edges of the batting to match the quilt, squaring up the corners if necessary. For a 7.5 mm ($\frac{1}{4}$") binding, trim the backing so that it extends 2–3 cm ($\frac{3}{4}$–1") past the quilt on all sides. Fold under to create a finished edge, and blind stitch the fold to the quilt front. Mitre corners as you come to them, trimming excess fabric that will lie under the fold if necessary.

Hanging sleeves

If your quilt will be displayed in a show or hung on a wall, sew a sleeve to its back.

1   Cut a 22.5 cm (9") wide piece of fabric about 5 cm (2") shorter than the width of the quilt.

2   Turn under each short end by 1.5 cm ($\frac{1}{2}$"). Press. Sew a straight or zigzag seam to secure the ends.

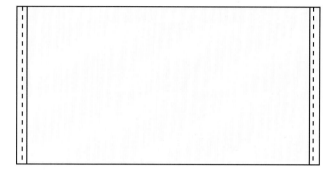

3   Place the wrong sides of the strip together lengthwise, aligning the raw edges. Sew together with a 1.5 cm ($\frac{1}{2}$") seam allowance. Press the seam open and centre it on the back of the tube.

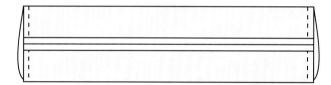

4   Centre the tube near the top edge of the quilt, seam against the backing. Use a blind stitch to sew the tube to the quilt around its top and bottom edges, and along the sides that touch the backing. Use a decorative curtain rod or dowel to mount the quilt on the wall.

Sleeve options

- Instead of attaching a sleeve after the quilt is complete, attach it along its top edge at the same time the binding is applied. The stronger seam is especially good for heavy quilts.
- If your hanging quilt is multi-directional, sew sleeves to two opposite sides. Alternate the hanging direction occasionally to reduce stress on any one portion of the quilt.

■ Miniature quilt with 3" blocks

- Another option is to make the label a more permanent part of the quilt by incorporating it into the backing, rather than just sewing it to the surface.

Washing the quilt

Half fill a bathtub with water no hotter than room temperature. Add Orvus Paste, or another mild soap. Fold large quilts into a shape that will fit the tub. Place them in the water and use your hands to force liquid through the layers. Drain the water and press as much liquid from the quilt as possible. Refill the tub with clean water and rinse. Repeat rinsing until all soap is gone.

Press as much liquid as possible from the quilt, using heavy towels to help absorb it. The best place to dry the quilt is flat on a bed, with a sheet of plastic placed on the mattress to protect it. Open the windows if possible, and turn a fan on the quilt. You want it to dry quickly, to avoid mildew and make colour transfer between patches less likely. *Never* dry a quilt on a clothes line: as the water migrates downward, it stretches the quilt and batting permanently out of shape.

When you give a quilt as a gift, give the lucky recipient care instructions too. Most people don't know that quilts shouldn't be washed in a washing machine, or dried in a dryer. Just a few words of caution will help to ensure that the quilt is a long-lasting gift

Labelling the quilt

- Sew a label with your name, date the quilt was made, and any other information you would like to include.
- Use permanent markers, or embroider the information.
- Appliqué the label to the quilt back.

Project 1: Starry Garden Wallhanging

U se quick-piecing techniques to sew this little wallhanging in record time. The quilt in the photograph is a scrappy version assembled with mostly floral fabrics. Star blocks were strip pieced in groups of five, then five different blocks were selected from the batch and alternated with a variation of the traditional Snowball block. The remaining blocks will be sewn into a co-ordinating bed quilt.

The instructions include everything you need to make a nine-block wallhanging. To make your own co-ordinating quilt, assemble more groups of blocks until you have the number required for your bed. Before you begin, make sure your machine is set up to sew an accurate 7.5 mm ($\frac{1}{4}$") seam allowance (see page 35).

Yardage

Star Blocks

- Light for background: 70 cm ($\frac{3}{4}$ yd)
- Medium for centre
  side squares: 20 cm ($\frac{3}{16}$ yd)
- Medium-dark for
  nine-patch: 20 cm ($\frac{1}{4}$ yd)
- Dark for star tips: 34 × 41 cm (14" × 17")
  rectangle

Snowball variation

- Medium-light for centres: 40 cm ($\frac{1}{3}$ yd)
- Medium for corners: 20 cm ($\frac{3}{16}$ yd)

Finishing

- Dark inner border: 20 cm ($\frac{1}{4}$ yd)
- Medium outer border: 50 cm ($\frac{1}{2}$ yd)
- Backing: 1.3 m ($1\frac{1}{4}$ yd)
- Binding: 480 running cm
  (172 running inches)
- Batting: piece 105 cm × 105 cm
  (42" × 42")

Cutting

Star blocks

Light fabric
- Twenty 6.5 cm ($2\frac{1}{2}$") squares
- One 34 cm × 41 cm (14 × 17") rectangle
- One 6.5 cm × 68 cm ($2\frac{1}{2}$" × 27") strip
- Two 6.5 cm × 34 cm ($2\frac{1}{2}$" × $13\frac{1}{2}$") strip

Medium fabric
- Twenty 6.5 cm ($2\frac{1}{2}$") medium centre side squares

Medium-dark fabric
- Two 6.5 cm × 68 cm ($2\frac{1}{2}$" × 27") strip
- One 6.5 cm × 34 cm ($2\frac{1}{2}$" × $13\frac{1}{2}$") strip

Dark fabric
- One 34 cm × 41 cm (14 × 17") rectangle

Snowball blocks

Medium-light fabric
- Four 31.5 cm × 31.5 cm ($10\frac{1}{2}$" × $10\frac{1}{2}$")

Medium fabric
- Twenty 6.5 cm × 6.5 cm ($2\frac{1}{2}$" × $2\frac{1}{2}$") medium squares

Dark inner border
- Four 4.5 cm × 105 cm ($1\frac{3}{4}$" × 42") strips

Medium outer border
- Four 10.5 cm × 105 cm (4" × 42") strips

Sewing the quilt

Make the star blocks

1   Use the grid method described on page 52 to assemble 40 identical half-square triangle units from the 34 cm × 41 cm (14" × 17") light and dark rectangles. Use a grid of four squares across and five down, with each square measuring 7.5 cm × 7.5 cm ($2\frac{7}{8}$" × $2\frac{7}{8}$"). Press seams towards the dark triangles. Each completed triangle square unit should measure 6.5 cm × 6.5 cm ($2\frac{1}{2}$" × $2\frac{1}{2}$").

2   Sew a 6.5 cm × 68 cm ($2\frac{1}{2}$" × 27") medium-dark strip to each side of a light background strip of the same length. Press seams toward the darker strips. Square up one end of the strip and cut ten 6.5 cm ($2\frac{1}{2}$") long segments from it.

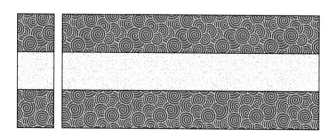

3 Sew a 6.5 cm × 34 cm ($2\frac{1}{2}$" × $13\frac{1}{2}$") light background strip to each side of a medium-dark strip of the same length. Press seams toward the darker strip. Square up one end of the strip and cut five 6.5 cm ($2\frac{1}{2}$") long segments from it.

4 Sew two segments from step 2 to a step 3 segment, matching seams carefully. Press seams towards the centre row. Repeat to make four more nine-patch units.

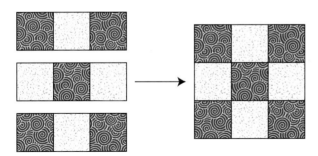

5 Arrange one nine-patch unit, eight star tips, four 6.5 cm ($2\frac{1}{2}$") background squares and four side-centre squares as shown.

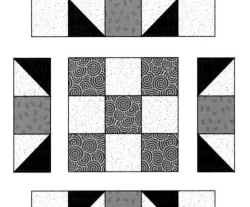

6 Sew together the outer vertical components of row 2. Press seams towards the centre square, then sew a unit to each side of the nine-patch centre. Press seams towards the nine-patch.

7 Sew together the components of rows 1 and 3. Press seam allowances away from the centre patch. Sew to the top and bottom of the block. Press final seams toward the nine-patch. Make four more identical blocks. Each should measure 30.5 cm ($10\frac{1}{2}$") square.

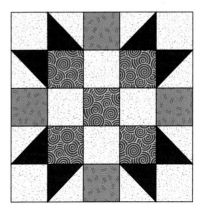

Make the Snowball blocks

8 Draw a diagonal line on the reverse side of each 6.5 cm ($2\frac{1}{2}$") medium square.

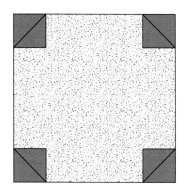

9   Place a marked square right-side down at the corner of a medium-light snowball square, aligning outer edges carefully. Sew a seam along the right-hand edge of the marked line (the edge nearest the corner). Repeat to sew squares to all four corners.

10 Transfer the Snowball block to your ironing board, just as it came from the machine, and set the seams by pressing them flat. Use scissors or rotary equipment to cut 7.5 mm ($\frac{1}{4}$") away from each seam, trimming off the excess tips of both squares. Carefully press seam allowances away from the corner. Make three more Snowball blocks.

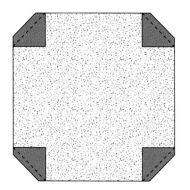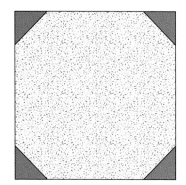

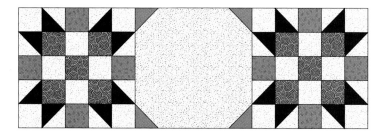

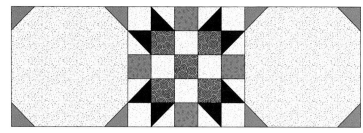

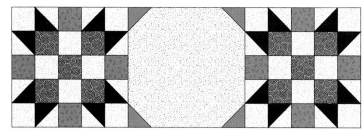

■ Assembling the quilt

Assembling the quilt

11 Arrange the blocks in three horizontal rows, each row containing three blocks. Begin with a star block, and alternate blocks from row to row.

12 Sew the components of each row together, matching seam intersections carefully. Press the seam allowances towards the Snowball blocks. Sew all rows together. Press the seam allowances towards the centre row.

Add the borders

13 Refer to page 93 for instructions about measuring for and sewing straight-sewn borders to the quilt. The measurements given are for crosswise grain border strips. Allow extra for lengthwise grain strips.

14 Sew the dark, 4.5 cm ($1\frac{3}{4}$") border to all sides of the quilt. Add the 10.5 cm (4") strips to complete the top.

Finish the quilt

15 Layer and baste the quilt, batting, and backing. Quilt as desired and bind. Refer to Chapter 11 for finishing instructions.

Project 2: Twisted tiles quilt

This small project can be put together quickly, because blocks are made from a combination of strip piecing and easy-to-sew squares. A slight twist is added to the 25 cm (10") blocks by sewing long triangles to their sides.

Finished size: approximately 60 × 60 cm (24 × 24")

Materials

- Light fabric: 0.6 m ($\frac{2}{3}$ yd)
- Medium-light fabric: 0.1 m ($\frac{1}{16}$ yd)
- Medium-dark fabric: 0.1 m ($\frac{1}{16}$ yd)
- Dark fabric: 0.3 m ($\frac{1}{3}$ yd)
- Backing: 0.8 m ($\frac{7}{8}$ yd)
- Batting: 75 × 75 cm (30" × 30") piece)
- Binding: 270 running cm (108 running inches)

Cutting

- Light: four 6.5 cm ($2\frac{1}{2}$") squares
  eight 6.25 × 46.5 cm ($2\frac{1}{2}$ × 16") rectangles
- Medium-light: one 6.5 × 105 cm ($2\frac{1}{2}$ × 42") strip
- Medium-dark: one 6.5 × 105 cm ($2\frac{1}{2}$ × 42") strip
- Dark: sixteen 11.5 ($4\frac{1}{2}$") squares

Sewing the quilt

1 Use a 7.5 mm ($\frac{1}{4}$") seam allowance to sew the medium-light strip lengthwise to the medium-dark strip. Press the seam towards the darker strip. Square up one end of the strip set, and cut sixteen 6.5 cm ($2\frac{1}{2}$") segments from it.

2 Sew a 11.5 cm ($4\frac{1}{2}$") dark square to each side of a segment from step 1. Press seam allowances towards the dark squares. Make seven more identical units.

3 Sew a segment from step 1 to each side of 6.5 cm ($2\frac{1}{2}$") light square. The darker portion of step 1 units should touch the light square. Press the seam allowances towards the light square. Make three more identical units.

4 Arrange the parts of a block into three rows. Position step 2 units with their small, darker square against the light square in the centre row. Sew the rows together, matching seams carefully. Press new seam allowances away from the centre row. Repeat to make three more blocks.

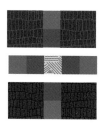 ▶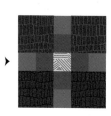

5 Cut four long, light rectangles in half once diagonally. Cut the remaining rectangles in half once diagonally, but along the opposite diagonal. Group like-triangles together.

6 Select four like-triangles. Align the 90° corner of one triangle with the top corner of a block, right sides together. If aligned correctly, the corners will match exactly, and the angled edge of the triangle will be to the left. Begin sewing at the corner, and end the seam at the block's midpoint. (Some seams are easier to sew with the triangle on the bottom.)

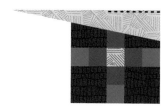

7 Add the second triangle to the block, again matching the 90° corners of both pieces. The tail of the second triangle should extend past the top, sewn edge of the first. Sew its entire length to the block. Press the seam allowance towards the triangle.

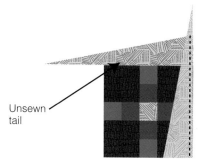

Unsewn tail

8   Add the third and fourth triangles in the same way, pressing seam allowances towards triangles after each seam. After sewing the last triangle, go back and complete the partial seam on the first. The tip of that triangle will be sewn to the wide edge of the last. Press the block.

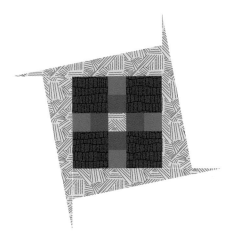

9   Place a large square ruler over the block. Position its upper right corner along a seam line. Twist the ruler until the same measurement intersects the remaining seam lines on the interior of the block. The sides of the block will not be parallel with the sides of the ruler. Ensure that the measurement leaves a minimum of 7.5 mm ($\frac{1}{4}$") seam allowance along each side of the inner block (leave a wider seam to make blocks appear to float on the background). Trim the right and top edges flush with the ruler.

10 Turn the block around and align the same dimension with the two trimmed edges. Trim the edges that extend past the ruler. Surround three more blocks with triangles.

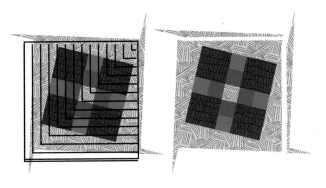

11 Since you used mirror image sets of triangles, blocks tilt in different directions. Arrange blocks to suit you, then sew together. Sandwich, quilt and bind using any technique you like.

Options

■ Cut long triangles from an assortment of scrappy fabrics.

■ This method makes it easy to assemble blocks of slightly different sizes, because adjustments can be made when triangles are trimmed. If blocks are very different in size, surround the smaller ones with an extra layer or two of triangles.

■ To calculate the rectangle length, add 14 cm (5$\frac{1}{2}$") to the unfinished block size. Width is your choice, but 6.25 cm (2$\frac{1}{2}$") is a good starting point. For narrower triangles, add extra length because seam allowance reduces the width that remains at their tips.

■ Cut all triangles along the same diagonal to make all blocks tilt in the same direction.

Templates

Please note that for all of the templates in this chapter the outer red line should be used for metric seams and the inner black line used for imperial seams.

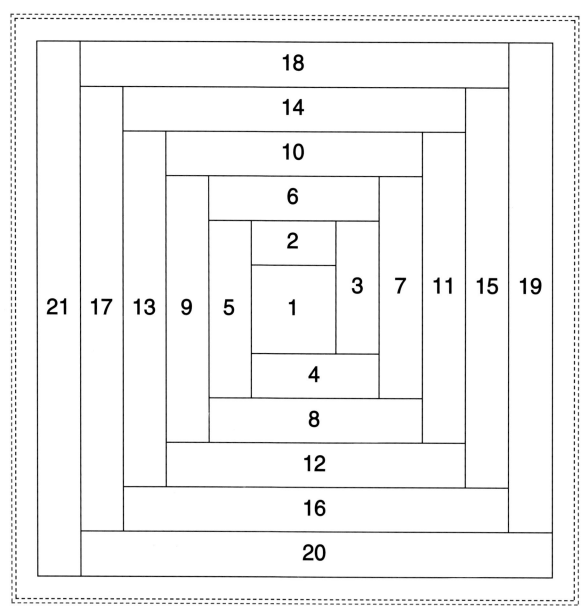

Foundation template, Log Cabin block

Basket block

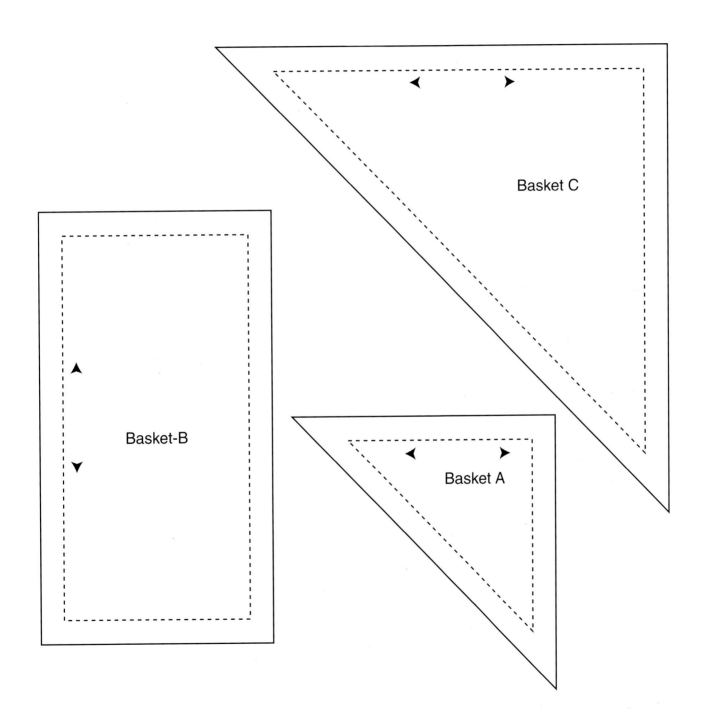

Basket C

Basket-B

Basket A

Bow-Tie templates

Drunkard's path

Hexagon template for English Paper Piecing

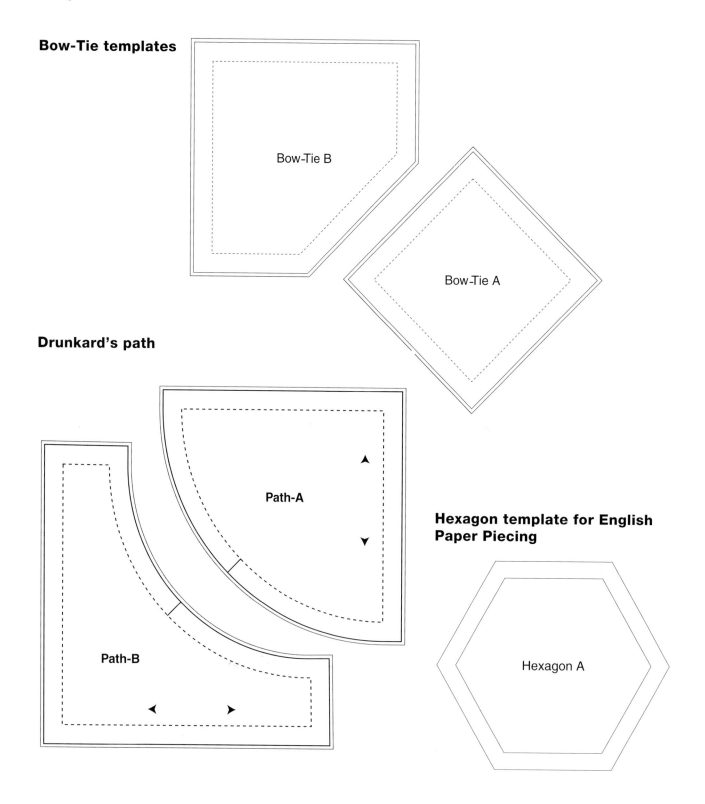

Bow-Tie B

Bow-Tie A

Path-A

Path-B

Hexagon A

Index

Index